LIKE A GIRL

Illustrated by Ayesha Broacha

ඬxi

REAL STORIES
FOR TOUGH KIDS

APARNA JAIN

Art Director: Ayesha Broacha

cntxt

First published by Context, an imprint of Westland Publications Private Limited in 2018

61, 2nd Floor, Silverline Building, Alapakkam Main Road, Maduravoyal, Chennai 600095

Westland, the Westland logo, Context and the Context logo are the trademarks of Westland Publications Private Limited, or its affiliates.

Text Copyright © Aparna Jain, 2018

ISBN: 9789387578470

For

Aditya *and* **Abhinav,**
more my brothers than cousins;

Nita *and* **Joanna,**
more my sisters than cousins-in-law:

parents of children to whom this book will be read.

·CONTENTS·

·PREFACE·

In 2016, I pledged money on a book on Kickstarter for my niece. That book is now a worldwide phenomenon. When it arrived, I loved it instantly and wondered why we didn't have a similar one for India. Around the same time, my sister-in-law, Nita, suggested I work on a book about concepts that parents and educators shy away from while talking to kids. I went to meet Karthika V.K. and Gautam Padmanabhan of Westland with a copy of *Good Night Stories for Rebel Girls*. They asked me to stop all other work and focus on this instead.

I realised early that the book would be neither as simple nor as short as *Rebel Girls*. India is diverse, and our landscape complex. The audience I wanted to write for was different and there could be no fixed format. Some stories would be simple, some would be tough, but every one of them would need to be told carefully and in some detail.

Choosing the icons was a bit of a nightmare. After drawing up an initial list with inputs from Oxfam India—who agreed to come on board as art sponsors—I thought I was set. Yet, every day I would message Karthika with a new name I had come across. My list quickly went from fifty to seventy-five.

Finally she wrote back, 'We are putting some women's worlds into these stories, not the entire world of women.' From then on, whenever I texted her a new name, she would text back, 'Volume two'.

Then there were debates about whether to include difficult figures like politicians, and whether to include material that may be considered sensitive by some. We wondered whether we were raising the bar too high when it came to our expectations of ethical conduct. But then I decided that I would tell the bad with the good. This would be a book that gives kids a chance to see the grey areas in the stories being told.

To add to the complexity, there was the element of art. I coerced my childhood friend Ayesha Broacha, who had worked with me on my first book, into becoming art director for the project. We commissioned twenty-six women artists from across the country. It became an online collective of sorts, with our youngest artists being only nineteen! And they were as engaged in this project as I was. Even now, I call it 'our book'.

When I fretted about the difficulties in some stories, my maami, Peggy Sood, an elementary school educator for over three decades (who also edited the initial drafts) told me, 'Make children step up to the writing and thoughts. Don't speak down to them.'

I tried to speak to everyone on my list. Some interviews did not pan out in time, some women preferred not to be part of the book, and there were others I couldn't contact. If some of the more obvious icons are missing, it is for one of these reasons.

You may disagree with the choice of women in the stories, but the hope is that it will propel discussion and debate. That the book will become a catalyst for greater engagement for children, parents and educators. I hope it sparks wonder, inspiration, conversation, anger, and maybe solutions.

The next time someone tries to insult you by saying 'just like a girl', remind them that as far as you are concerned, it is a compliment!

Aparna Jain
April 2018

Illustrated by Tara Anand

· SULTAN RAZIA ·

Delhi's Monarch

Seven hundred years ago, Sultan Iltutmish, the ruler of the Delhi Sultanate, had a daughter whom he named Razia. Her birth was celebrated throughout the kingdom.

As a child, Razia learnt to ride a horse and to use a bow and arrow. Her father taught her how to deal with people and, more importantly, how to manage a kingdom. He would even let her ride with him when he went to battle so she could learn the art of war.

One day, Iltutmish had to leave Delhi for Gwalior. He left young Razia in charge of the kingdom. When he returned and heard what a brilliant job she had done, he announced that she would inherit the kingdom after his death. He said that she was worth twenty sons! This decision made a lot of people angry because they didn't think it was a woman's place to rule.

When Iltutmish died, the nobles in the court made her brother Ruknuddin the king. Ruknuddin was lazy and ineffectual, and the kingdom suffered greatly under his rule. After a few months, Razia decided to do something about it. Dressed in red (the colour of protest), she went to the mosque where many people had gathered for their Friday prayers.

She spoke to them earnestly, promising that she would do what her father had wanted—become the ruler of the kingdom and help them get rid of the indolent, selfish sultan. With the army's backing, she compelled her brother to hand over the kingdom to her, its rightful ruler.

Razia stopped wearing a veil and women's clothes and started to dress in a man's tunic and headdress to look like an ordinary soldier. This shocked many people, but Razia focused on ruling the kingdom instead of being affected by people's opinions of her. She also refused to be called Razia Sultana because that would have implied she was the wife of a ruler, when in fact she *was* the ruler.

Sultan Razia, as she was called, ruled the kingdom well for four years. But then one of her governors, a man named Malik Altunia, who was also her childhood friend, decided that he wanted to rule the kingdom. He rebelled against Razia, defeated her, and took her prisoner. Razia wasn't entirely powerless, though. She agreed to marry Altunia and they left for Delhi together. But when they reached there, they found that her half-brother Bahram had taken over the kingdom. Razia and Altunia fought bravely, but she was killed in the battle that followed. Since she was dressed as a soldier, no one realised she was dead until much later.

You can still see Sultan Razia's grave in Old Delhi near Turkman Gate, amidst a warren of narrow lanes and shops. There is a grave next to hers—the locals call the two Razia-Shazia—but no one knows who it belongs to.

Sultan Razia is still remembered as Delhi's only woman monarch.

●●

· CHAND BIBI ·

Warrior Queen

Chand Bibi was fourteen when her father, Hussain Nizam Shah of Ahmednagar (in present-day Maharashtra), got her married to Ali Adil Shah of Bijapur in 1554. In those days, rulers used marriage as a way of expanding their territory and strengthening their kingdoms. This marriage, too, was exactly that—an alliance between two kingdoms.

As Chand Bibi grew older, she rode with her husband, accompanying him everywhere—from hunts and battles to visits to the new lands they had conquered. She was a brave and generous woman and did everything in her power to help the people in her kingdom find support and justice.

Although Chand Bibi didn't wear a veil as was the custom in those days, she kept her face partly covered. She was exceptionally talented; she played the veena, sang beautifully, and even composed her own music. She could also speak a number of languages—Persian, Arabic, Turkish, Marathi and Kannada, among others.

Chand Bibi's husband died when she was still very young. Since they had no children, her husband had named his nephew Ibrahim Adil Shah as the heir to the throne, with Chand Bibi as the young king's guardian. Chand Bibi now spent most of her time educating Ibrahim, leaving her minister, Kamil Khan, to manage the affairs of the kingdom. The power-hungry Kamil Khan—and every one of the ministers who came after him—tried to seize the throne but failed.

Meanwhile, the Mughal emperor Akbar was in the process of expanding his empire and wanted to annexe Ahmednagar. Chand Bibi refused to give up her kingdom without a fight and asked the other kings in the Deccan for help.

Illustrated by Priya Kuriyan

Akbar's forces surrounded the Ahmednagar fort and destroyed a part of it. Against all odds, Chand Bibi and her army managed to defend the fort and the Mughal forces had no choice but to retreat. People started calling her Chand Sultana after that battle.

In 1599, Akbar's son Daniyal attacked Ahmednagar, this time with a larger army, and was able to lay siege to the fort. Chand Bibi fought bravely but was forced to reach an agreement with Daniyal: she and her nephew would leave the kingdom forever, in return for which he would spare the lives of her subjects. However, a treacherous minister named Hamid Khan spread a rumour that she had ceded the throne to Akbar in a secret deal, and her own soldiers killed her in a fit of anger.

A few months after she died, the Mughals conquered Ahmednagar.

Chand Bibi is remembered today as one of the greatest warriors to stand between the Deccan and the mighty Mughal forces.

Illustrated by Aparajita Ninan

·RANI LAKSHMIBAI·

Battling the British

Manikarnika was born in Kashi. When she was four years old, her mother died. Her father, an advisor in the court of the Peshwa of Bithur, made sure Manu was taught everything that the boys in the household were, including sword fighting, horse riding and mallakhamba.

When Manu was fourteen, she was married to the Maharaja of Jhansi—Gangadhar Rao Newalkar—and renamed Lakshmi, after the goddess of wealth. Even though the women in the court lived in separate quarters and always behind a veil, young, feisty Rani Lakshmibai continued to practise with the sword and taught many other women to fight as well.

A few years later, Lakshmibai had a baby boy, who died not many days after he was born. At that time, the British had a cunning strategy for seizing new territories in India. If a ruler died without an heir, his kingdom would automatically be added to the British empire. In 1853, the Raja and Lakshmibai adopted a three-year-old boy named Damodar in the presence of a British officer. Unfortunately, the Raja died the next day. While the British professed to admire Lakshmibai and her ability to take charge of the kingdom, they refused to recognise her adopted son and demanded that Jhansi be given to them.

In 1857, the first ever rebellion against the British in north India broke out in Meerut. When Lakshmibai heard of it, she asked the local British officer if she could keep a small army of soldiers for her own protection. He agreed. The British then asked her to manage Jhansi on their behalf till they were able to send their soldiers. She consented and was declared their regent.

When the soldiers finally arrived, Lakshmibai refused to hand over Jhansi to them. She defended the city as best she could, but the British forces were too strong. Finally, her advisors suggested that she leave Jhansi. So she strapped twelve-year-old Damodar to her back and rode bravely out into the night.

Lakshmibai and her band of soldiers camped out in Gwalior. She joined forces with Tantia Tope, another rebel leader and her childhood friend, and they fought the British together.

In a battle in 1858, Lakshmibai was severely wounded. She asked her soldiers to take her son to safety and then rode away to a quiet place. As she lay dying, a sadhu came up to her. She spoke to him and made him promise that he would not allow her body to be touched by a British soldier. When the courageous queen finally died, he had her cremated.

You can visit Rani Lakshmibai's memorial at Phool Bagh in Gwalior.

• •

·SAVITRIBAI PHULE·

Rebel Reformer

Savitri was getting married to Jotirao Phule, who like her was from the Shudra community.

The Shudras were considered to be 'low caste' and were shunned and discriminated against by the other castes. Shudras rarely had the opportunity to study, but Jotirao's mother had insisted he get an education. He, in turn, insisted that Savitri should study too. For six years, he was her teacher. Subsequently she went to a school in Pune.

A few years later, the Phules set up their own school. In the courtyard of their house, they held night classes for the workers in their neighbourhood. Their friend Fatima Shaikh joined them, and together they taught blacksmiths, cobblers, labourers and vessel makers.

In 1848, they started a school for girls in Bhidewada, Pune. There were just nine students in the first class, and they were all from the Shudra–Atishudra community.

Every day, as young Savitribai walked to school, people would throw cow dung and mud at her. They were angry that she was teaching young girls from the 'lower castes'. In their view, these communities did not deserve an education. Savitribai started carrying an extra sari to change into when she reached school. Before going home, she would change back into the dirty sari.

In those days, if a woman's husband died, her head was shaved so she could be identified as a widow. Even little girls whose husbands had died had to get their heads shaved. Savitribai campaigned for an end to this practice and organised a barbers' strike in Pune and Bombay.

Infanticide or the killing of babies at birth was another age-old evil. If a woman gave birth after she became a widow, her baby was killed.

Illustrated by Bhavya Kumar

10

Savitribai started a home to provide shelter to widows so they could deliver their babies safely. Thirty-five babies were born in the home which was later converted to a hospital.

Savitribai and Jotirao themselves adopted a Brahmin widow's child. That boy grew up to marry a girl from the Mali community. It was probably one of the earliest inter-caste marriages recorded in British India.

Upon Jotirao's death, their son Yashwant insisted his mother light the pyre. Another act that defied tradition.

Savitribai died of the plague at the age of sixty-six. There are many who feel that her birthday—3 January—should be celebrated as Teachers' Day. After all, she was among the first women to set up schools for the education of Dalits and the underprivileged in modern India.

Illustrated by Sanchita Jain

·RUKHMABAI RAUT·

Changemaker

It was 1875, and Rukhma was being married to a nineteen-year-old boy named Dadaji Bhikaji. Child marriage was an accepted practice in India in those days. Sometimes children as young as two were married. According to custom, Rukhma would stay in her own home till she was old enough to live with her husband and his family.

Rukhma's stepfather, Dr Sakharam Arjun, was a doctor in Bombay. Her own father had died when she was two and her mother had remarried. Her stepfather encouraged her to study and it was because of him that she started learning English.

A few years after Rukhma attained puberty, her husband demanded that she move into his house. But when she went to meet him, she found him to be incredibly lazy—he didn't want to work or study further. Disgusted, she refused to go and live with him. Her mother and grandfather were upset with her decision, but her stepfather supported her and urged her to continue her studies.

Eventually, Dadaji Bhikaji went to court to demand that Rukhmabai move in with him. The court gave twenty-two-year-old Rukhmabai a choice: she could go to her husband's home, or to jail. Rukhmabai was a brave young woman. She declared that she would prefer to go to jail. She said she had not agreed to the marriage. At eleven, she had been too young to make such an important decision about her future.

Rukhmabai had no idea that her defiance would lead to one of the most significant legal pronouncements of the time: the judge decided he could not force a woman to go to her husband's home when she had not consented to the marriage.

People were deeply divided over the issue. Some, who were progressive and understood the injustice of child marriage, welcomed the decision. But there were many others who thought it was an attack on Indian culture.

Bhikaji's lawyers appealed to the courts again and the case went on for some time. Finally, it was decided that Rukhmabai's marriage was valid. But she refused to go to her husband's home and stated again that she was willing to face a jail sentence instead.

During this time, Rukhmabai wrote long, detailed letters about the terrible practice of child marriage and her own situation to the *Times of India*, signing off as 'A Hindu Woman'. Most other newspapers covered the case too.

Encouraged by the response, Rukhmabai found the courage to keep the battle going. She wrote to Queen Victoria (India was under British rule then), asking her to intervene. The queen overruled the courts, dissolved the marriage, and saved Rukhmabai from going to jail. This was an important moment for women's rights in India.

In 1889, a few women supporters got together to pay for Rukhmabai to go to England and study medicine. After five years, she came back as India's first practicing woman doctor. Despite her qualifications, her life was no cakewalk. It was sheer grit and perseverance that allowed her to sustain her practice for thirty-five years and become chief medical officer of a hospital, first in Surat and then in Rajkot.

Rukhmabai continued her battle against child marriage and purdah through her writings. When she died at the age of ninety-one, her house was converted into a school, just as she had wished.

••

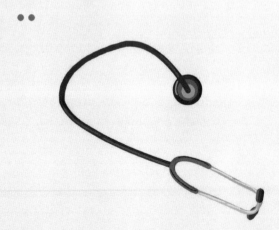

· MUTHULAKSHMI REDDI ·

Doctor–Legislator

It was the year 1890. Four-year-old Lakshmi was learning the Tamil alphabet in her courtyard school. Lakshmi's father was the principal of a college and a disciplinarian with definite ideas about his daughter's future. He wanted her to study just enough to be able to manage the milk and dhobi accounts at home. But slowly, with some help from others, Lakshmi started learning English on the side.

When Lakshmi was ten years old, her mother wanted her to get married, but she insisted on going to school. One of Lakshmi's teachers supported her, and her father gave in. She was the only girl in the whole school. The school authorities hung a large sheet in the classroom, separating her from the boys. When it was time to leave, the teacher would ring a bell. That was the signal for Lakshmi to leave the class; the boys left only after she was gone. Later, Lakshmi's father engaged a home tutor for her and then he started teaching her himself.

Lakshmi wanted to go to college, but the only college in the area refused her admission because she was a girl. Her father appealed to the raja of the province, who was a liberal man. He granted her a scholarship and declared that girls who passed the tenth grade should be allowed to go to college. And so Lakshmi joined college—again, she was the only girl there.

Many in the village were upset about her going to college, not only because of her gender, but also because of her caste: she was the daughter of a devadasi. Some even said that they would not let their sons study in Maharajah College if she was admitted!

Lakshmi went on to graduate top of her class and was soon on her way to Madras Medical College.

Illustrated by Priya Kuriyan

Lakshmi's teachers in medical school were British. They too believed that women were not capable of studying medicine. Some professors did not even allow women to sit in their classes.

Soon it was exam time. The answer papers that the students handed in carried no names, just numbers to identify them. There was one teacher of whom everyone was terrified—Major Niblock. Before handing out the exam results, he mentioned to his colleagues that one of his students had scored 100 per cent. When he realised it was Lakshmi, he jumped out of his seat and shouted joyfully to the class, 'A lady student, Miss Muthulakshmi Ammal, has got cent per cent!'

In 1912, Muthulakshmi left Madras Medical College as the first woman medical graduate in India—and with honours. Her photograph was in all the newspapers and she received several congratulatory letters, including one from Sarojini Naidu. Hospitals across the country sent her offers to join them. But Muthulakshmi decided to remain in Madras and became the first woman house-surgeon at the Government Hospital for Women and Children.

A few years later, Muthulakshmi's younger sister was diagnosed with cancer, a disease that was thought to affect only older people. Not many options were available then for treatment, and her sister died. This was a turning point in Muthulakshmi's life. She decided that she would specialise in the study of cancer, and moved to London with her family on a government scholarship.

On her return from London, she became the first woman legislator in British India. She introduced many important bills, including one to abolish the devadasi system. When the bill became law, many women were freed. But many others were thrown out of their homes. Muthulakshmi realised there was no safe place for these women to live and learn new skills. So she set up an institution that took in widows, single mothers and other women with the purpose of educating them. Over 170 women now live and study at the Avvai Home.

Soon after India became independent, Dr Reddi decided to start a cancer hospital in Madras. When she approached the chief minister for land, he asked her why she wanted a hospital for patients who would only die on her. She was shocked at the ignorance and apathy of the administration. Nevertheless, she managed to establish a small unit with twelve beds.

Today, the Cancer Institute in Chennai has 450 beds, of which 60 per cent are for the underprivileged. This is indeed a tribute to the legend and vision of Dr Muthulakshmi Reddi.

••

·RUKMINI DEVI ARUNDALE·

Cultural Icon

Rukku was listening to her father attentively. He was sitting on a mat, reading the Ramayana aloud by the light of a lantern. This was how her father entertained her and her siblings in the late evenings.

At school, Rukmini was often shocked at the way her teachers disciplined the children. The slightest transgression could earn them a severe caning. Once, her class teacher chained a boy's leg to a heavy log for coming late to school. Rukmini complained to her father, who immediately wrote a letter to the dewan. The dewan responded by sending a letter to all the schools in the area, forbidding them from using corporal punishment.

After some time the family moved to Madras and Rukmini's father joined the Theosophical Society. That was how Rukmini met the theosophist and scholar George Arundale and married him. They travelled together for various theosophical conventions all over the world. As she travelled, Rukmini took in as much as she could of the music, theatre and dance in the places she visited.

Once, Rukmini and the legendary ballerina Anna Pavlova happened to be travelling on the same ship. Rukmini had seen her perform several times and been mesmerised by her. She told her, 'I wish I could dance like you.' Anna generously offered to teach Rukmini ballet. She also advised her to explore her own dance culture.

But Rukmini was not allowed to watch dance performances in Madras. In those days, there was a stigma attached to dance. It was performed only by devadasis.

On Rukmini's insistence, her brothers took her to see a Sadir dance performance by two devadasi sisters. Fascinated by their skill and the complexity of the dance, she became determined to learn it. She

50⁰⁰

RUKMINI DEVI ARUNDALE

INDIA

Illustrated by Sudeepti Tucker

trained under two well-known teachers and also studied the *Natya Shastra*. Finally, at the age of thirty-one, she was ready for a public performance. Though she had only invited her friends, several hundred people turned up. Most of the audience thought the performance was vulgar and were quite shocked by it. Rukmini remained unperturbed. And thus the modern dance form of Bharatanatyam was born.

With the encouragement of some eminent scholars, musicologists and artists, Rukmini set up a centre for arts and culture named Kalakshetra in 1936. It started small—one student, one teacher. At that time, families did not allow their children to learn dance because it was considered immoral. Nevertheless, in time, the school grew.

All her life, Rukmini was a vegetarian and a supporter of animal rights. One day, she was at a train station when a caged monkey grabbed the edge of her sari. It seemed to her that it was asking for her help. One thing led to another and eventually she became instrumental in the passing of the Prevention of Cruelty to Animals Act.

In 1952, Rukmini became the first woman to be nominated to the Rajya Sabha. In 1977, when President Fakhruddin Ali Ahmed passed away while still in office, Prime Minister Morarji Desai invited her to become the President of India, but she refused. She believed she was born to serve the arts.

Rukmini choreographed over thirty dance dramas in her lifetime. The most famous of these was based on the stories from the Ramayana that her father used to tell her when she was little.

Rukmini died at the age of eighty-two. There are many who say that the students of Kalakshetra are the best exponents of Bharatanatyam. There are others who are critical of the way in which she appropriated the Sadir dance form and 'refined' it to suit middle-class morality.

● ●

Illustrated by Tanya Eden

22

·DEVIKA RANI·

First Lady of Indian Cinema

As a young girl, Devika had many interests. She went to a boarding school in the English countryside in the early 1900s, after which she studied at the Royal Academy of Dramatic Art, a school which trained students in acting, production and theatre. She also studied at the Royal Academy of Music, and then trained in textile engineering. She was immensely talented and was soon designing costumes, backdrops and sets for an English film producer.

While still in London, Devika met Himanshu Rai, a lawyer-turned-filmmaker from Calcutta. Himanshu was impressed by Devika's skills and convinced her to become an assistant set designer on his silent film, *A Throw of Dice*. A few years later, they came back to India to make another film, *Karma*. Devika played the lead role opposite Himanshu in the film. She even sang a bilingual (English–Hindi) song in it.

Now married, Himanshu and Devika went to Berlin to edit the film. While there, she also apprenticed in make-up, set design and costume design, and soaked up everything she could.

Although *Karma* didn't do well in India, its English version premiered successfully in London. Devika was applauded for her performance, diction and charm. She was now a star.

Back in India, Himanshu founded a film studio called Bombay Talkies. It was the first fully equipped studio in the country and was located in Malad in Bombay, which was then a distant suburb. It became a launch pad for many artistes.

Devika herself acted in a number of films including *Achhut Kannya*. She was responsible for recruiting singers and actors and managing their costumes. She was also great at spotting new talent. Once, when she went to the market, she saw a shy-looking boy at a fruit stall. He was the fruit seller's son. She found his face interesting and gave him her visiting card. When he came to the studio, she changed his name from Yusuf Khan to Dilip Kumar and launched his career in the film industry.

A few years later, when Himanshu died, Devika stepped up to run the studio, becoming the first woman in India to take over a production house. She was familiar with most aspects of the work by now and went on to make a string of successful films.

In 1945, Devika sold the studio and married a Russian painter named Svetoslav Roerich whom she had met a year earlier. They settled in Bangalore on a large estate where Devika developed and managed a perfume export business.

Devika Rani passed away at the age of eight-six. In her lifetime, she received a number of awards for her contribution to the film industry. Today, she is hailed as the first lady of Indian cinema.

• •

AMRITA SHER-GIL

Rebel Artist

Amri leaned over the bathtub, standing on tiptoe. Her Hungarian mother, Marie-Antoinette, was giving Amri's little sister Indira a bath, and Amri was throwing her own little toys—fish, ducks and frogs—into the bathtub for Indira to play with. Amri loved animals and she called her baby sister all sorts of affectionate animal names while growing up.

When Amrita was five, her favourite activity was colouring the toys she saw around her. She hated colouring books. Why should she colour pictures that other people had drawn for her?

In 1921, faced with the fear of political hardship and economic instability in Hungary, Amrita's father, Umrao, decided to move the family back to India. Amrita was a shy, serious girl who preferred to sit quietly in the company of adults rather than play with other children. Observing her interest in art, her mother enrolled her for classes. But Amrita hated the art teacher, who wanted her to draw perfectly and made her repeat her sketches again and again. She continued to draw in her own unique style.

Three years later, Marie-Antoinette took the girls to Italy. Amrita joined a convent school, but she found the atmosphere there stifling. One day she happened to draw a nude woman and the horrified nuns wanted to expel her. The family eventually returned to India, and she was admitted to a Catholic boarding school in Simla.

Amrita continued to rebel against the system. For one, she refused to attend the morning Mass, which was mandatory for all students. Once, she wrote a letter to her parents describing how much she disliked any constraints. The head nun read the letter and threatened to expel her. Amrita would write letters all her life to people she cared about, inadvertently documenting her life.

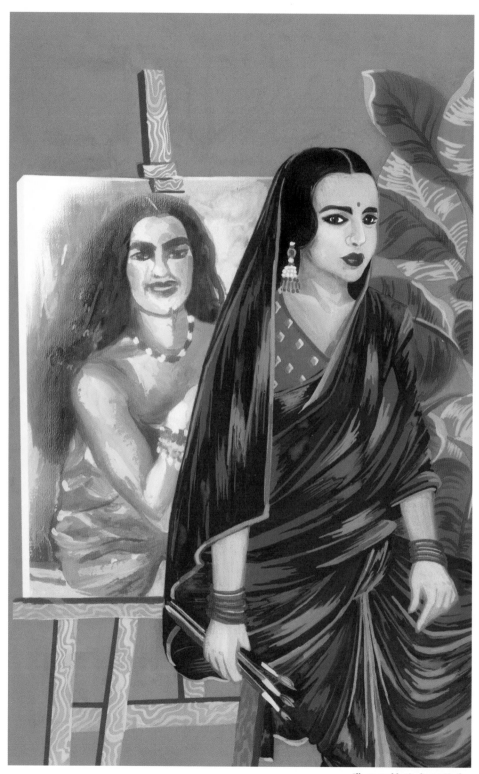

Illustrated by Sudeepti Tucker

When Amrita was sixteen, a friend suggested to her parents that they send her to Paris so she could develop her talent further. The whole family sailed to Paris, and Amrita went to the acclaimed École des Beaux-Arts, which had trained many great artists. She studied there for a few years and was fascinated by the little cafes and the people on the streets of the city. After a while, she began to seek out the unconventional. She spent more time in the back streets and the Latin Quarter, and started painting the poor and homeless. She made many charcoal sketches and then began working with oils. She did more than sixty paintings between 1930 and 1932.

Amrita wanted to strike out on her own and so decided to go back to Simla, away from the influence of the West. She also decided that she would only wear saris—she found them much more elegant than Western clothing. Her saris were always in deep, beautiful colours and she paired them with striking blouses and chunky earrings. Wherever she went, she made an impression.

Amrita travelled with the artist Barada Ukil to Ajanta and Ellora and many cities in southern India. Inspired, she went back to Simla and did some of her best work: the paintings in the South Indian Trilogy.

Amrita wrote a number of letters to her cousin and childhood friend Victor Egan—who was now a doctor in Hungary—about her work, her paintings and her life; her letters were like a diary. Against the wishes of her parents, Victor and she married in Hungary, and later moved into her cousin's home in Saraya in Uttar Pradesh.

Victor eventually moved to Lahore to set up a practice and Amrita joined him there. Two weeks before she was supposed to have an exhibition, in December 1941, she fell ill and died within a few days. She was only twenty-eight years old.

Amrita's paintings have influenced generations of Indian artists. Many of them are considered to be national art treasures by the Indian government, and cannot be sent out of the country. Today, the National Gallery of Modern Art houses over a hundred of her amazing artworks.

Illustrated by Sudeepti Tucker

·HOMAI VYARAWALLA·

Lady with the Lens

Homai was sitting amidst bottles of paint, brushes and a giant canvas, watching her father, Dossabhai, who was in the middle of a rehearsal. Dossabhai was part of a travelling Parsi theatre troupe, and the paint was being used to create the backdrop for his plays. The family was not affluent, so these were Homai's only toys.

Homai used to watch the actors at work every day. Since the language of Dossabhai's plays was Urdu, she learnt to speak it well. One day, when an actor forgot her lines, Homai got up and declaimed the part perfectly. That was the last time she was allowed to be present at the rehearsals. In those days 'good girls' did not take part in theatre.

When Homai was seven, her mother moved the three children to Bombay. Homai, who only spoke Urdu, was sent to a school where everyone had to speak English. When she left home for school, her mother would make her wear a mathibanu, the Parsi headscarf; a sudreh, a slip that stuck out from under her blouse; and a kusti, the Parsi sacred thread. As soon as she was out of sight, she would pull off the mathibanu and stuff it into her bag, then fold the sudreh into her blouse. She didn't want to feel like an old woman. But she remembered to pull the slip out and wear her headscarf before she got back home.

At school, Homai made a good friend, Manekshaw, whom she eventually married. Manekshaw shot photographs of Bombay for a famous magazine. Homai shared his love for photography and would often assist him. It was unheard of then, for a woman to be a professional photographer, so her work was published under his name—or rather, his initials, MJV.

In 1942, Homai started work at the British Information Services. She was their first woman photographer. She insisted on wearing a sari to work because she felt that it was important to show she was a woman in a man's world. She travelled widely and adapted to the toughest of situations without demur.

Thirteen is considered to be an unlucky number by many people, but Homai considered it lucky. She was born in 1913, she met Manekshaw when she was thirteen, and the license plate number of her car was DLD 13. Many years later, a film made on her was titled *Dalda 13*.

Around the time of India's independence, Homai started taking photos depicting the transfer of power from Britain to India. She documented the ceremonies before Independence, which included the historic unfurling of the Indian flag at Red Fort on 16 August. Thousands of people were out on the streets celebrating. She photographed it all. Her picture of British soldiers leaving the country by sea from the Gateway of India became especially famous.

Homai's photographs are considered important records of the birth of independent India. You can see some of them at the National Gallery of Modern Art even today.

LAKSHMI SAHGAL &
MRINALINI SARABHAI

The Swaminadhan Sisters

Mrinal stared at the full plate of food in front of her in terror. Her elder sister, Lakshmi, watched her anxiously—she knew Mrinal was a fussy eater. 'We do not waste food. You have to eat whatever is placed in front of you' was something their mother said before every meal. She had a stick to rap Mrinal's knuckles with, if any food was left on her plate. When their mother stepped out for a minute, Lakshmi ran over to Mrinal's side of the table, pushed the food from her sister's plate on to her own and polished it off! She did this whenever she got the chance.

Mrinalini had a difficult relationship with her mother, who she felt was often mean and harsh to her. She was, however, her father's pet. Mrinal was so skinny as a child that her father once promised her a gold sovereign for every pound she put on. She never won a single one!

Mrinalini absorbed all that she heard. One day, when she was asked to entertain her mother's best friend, the eleven-year-old turned to Mrs Sen and, to her astonishment, asked her whether she wanted to discuss art or politics!

Mrinalini was always a little frail, so she was sent to Switzerland to study. Meanwhile, Lakshmi, who wanted to be a doctor, went to medical college in Madras.

Because of her mother's contacts as a Congress leader, Lakshmi met many interesting people including Suhasini Chattopadhyay, the first woman to join the Communist Party of India. She was fascinated by Suhasini's stories of the Russian Revolution. Generous and caring as she was, these stories encouraged her to 'steal' food and clothes from home for poor patients in the hospital.

Illustrated by Ayesha Broacha

Shortly afterwards, Lakshmi went to Singapore and started a clinic where she treated the families of poor Indian migrant workers. In 1942, the Indian National Army (INA) or Azad Hind Fauj was founded, with the intention of liberating India from the British. One of the first to join was Prem Sahgal, a dashing young officer from the British Indian Army. He met Lakshmi in Singapore, and the two became friends.

When Netaji Subhas Chandra Bose went to Singapore to take over the leadership of the INA, he met Lakshmi and asked her if she would help him establish a women's regiment in the INA. The next day, she closed her clinic and started recruiting and training women soldiers—mostly from the poor and middle-class families of the region. The Rani of Jhansi Regiment grew to be 1200 strong.

The Ranis (as the women in the regiment were called) and Lakshmi came face-to-face with the many horrors of war, but they confronted them bravely. Lakshmi was placed under house arrest. She returned to India in 1946, and soon afterwards, Prem, who had also been arrested, was released. They got married and settled in Kanpur.

Lakshmi joined the Communist Party of India (Marxist) (CPI-M) and was nominated in 2002 to contest the Presidential election. She did not win.

She continued to practice as a doctor for the poor until the age of ninety-seven, when she died of a heart attack. Kanpur, it is said, had never seen a funeral procession like hers.

And what of Mrinalini? When she came back from Switzerland, she wanted to learn dance. But her mother had no idea where to send her. Mrinalini finally went to learn Bharatanatyam at the Kalakshetra academy set up by Rukmini Devi Arundale, who was her mother's friend. After a few years she went to Santiniketan, where she truly blossomed. She was asked to perform in front of Rabindranath Tagore, who cast her in one of his plays. Shortly afterwards, Mrinalini's mother decided to travel to America and took Mrinalini with her. When they came back to India, Mrinalini went to Bangalore, where she performed a dance drama with the famous dancer Ramgopal.

It was here that she met Vikram Sarabhai, a young scientist whom she had known briefly as a teenager. They got married in 1942 and moved to Ahmedabad, where Vikram's family lived.

Mrinalini felt lonely in Ahmedabad. Not only did she not speak Gujarati, but she could barely eat the food. Vikram was always busy at work. One day, they were attending a Quit India rally when a soldier, mistaking Vikram's camera for a gun, lobbed a tear gas shell in their direction. It hit Mrinalini and blinded her in one eye. Although she was devastated, Mrinalini continued with her dance performances. Not once did she stumble or fall off the stage.

It took a year for Mrinalini to find the right doctor and treatment for her eye. Sometime later, when Vikram and she moved to Bangalore, she started a dance troupe called Darpana. When they moved back to Ahmedabad, she took the entire troupe with her. The Gujarat audiences, who were mostly used to folk dances, were fascinated by their performances.

Mrinalini travelled widely; she and her troupe performed in theatres around the world to packed audiences. She choreographed more than 300 dance dramas. As long as she lived, Mrinalini remained deeply committed to making dance accessible to people everywhere.

• •

Illustrated by Rae Zachariah

· SHAH BANO BEGUM ·

Catalyst for Change

Shah Bano Begum was married to her cousin, Ahmed Khan, an advocate in Indore, when she was very young. Her father was a conservative police constable, and Shah Bano was never sent to school. Marriage didn't make things better—she remained confined to her house.

After fourteen years of marriage and five children with Shah Bano, Ahmed Khan married another cousin—Halima Begum—and had two more children.

However, Halima was not happy living with Shah Bano and her family. In 1975, after forty-three years of marriage, Ahmed Khan threw Shah Bano out of their home. She had no means of supporting herself and moved in with her son.

In April 1978, on the insistence of her son, Shah Bano filed a petition in a court in Indore, asking for a maintenance amount of Rs 500 a month from her husband. In November 1978, Ahmed Khan divorced her. By uttering the word 'talaq' three times, a Muslim man could legally divorce his wife. Shah Bano was sixty-two years old then.

Muslim Personal Law requires that the divorced wife be paid mehr and iddat for three months. Ahmed Khan claimed that he had paid Shah Bano a sum of Rs 3000 and so his responsibility had been fulfilled. The district court, however, ordered him to pay her a monthly maintenance of Rs 25 a month. Shah Bano had never worked for a living—how was she to support herself for the rest of her life?

After Shah Bano filed another application in the High Court of Madhya Pradesh, the payment increased to Rs 179.20 every month.

Unhappy with the judgement, Ahmed Khan filed an appeal in the Supreme Court. The case was heard by a bench of five judges, led by Justice Y.B. Chandrachud. On 25 April 1985, a historic decision was reached. Shah Bano was to be paid a monthly maintenance of Rs 500 for the rest of her life.

Progressive Muslim women and activists were delighted, but conservative Muslims were enraged. How could any court decide what was good for them? How could it interfere with their religious practices? Shah Bano faced heavy opposition from her community when she returned to her son's home. Rallies were held across the country protesting the decision.

The then prime minister of India, Rajiv Gandhi, was perturbed. Many Muslim organisations said they only believed in the Shariyat (laws based on the Quran) and would protest against this decision by the Supreme Court. In 1986, he used his party's Lok Sabha majority to pass the Muslim Women (Protection of Rights on Divorce) Act in Parliament. It diluted the Shah Bano judgement and the decision of the Supreme Court.

Meanwhile, Shah Bano was under intense pressure to withdraw her case. She was also constantly ill. Eventually she succumbed and a press conference was organised. She put her thumbprint on a document that demanded the Supreme Court withdraw its verdict since it interfered with Muslim Law.

Shah Bano died at age seventy-five of a brain haemorrhage.

In August 2017, nearly forty years after she had filed her original petition for relief, the Supreme Court finally declared the act of triple talaq or instant divorce unconstitutional.

• •

·M.S. SUBBULAKSHMI·

Matchless Melody

Kunjamma was sitting on a window ledge in her house in the temple city of Madurai. Her neighbours had acquired a new gramophone and Kunjamma loved to listen to the music they played. Since she was born into the devadasi tradition, she and her siblings were always surrounded by music. While their mother—a veena player—did not teach her children formally, she did give them some basic instruction. For the rest, they learnt by listening and watching.

Young Kunjamma used to pick up the tanpuras in the house and tune them. She would listen to songs on the gramophone and sing them back without a mistake. Her mother noticed Kunjamma's unusual quality of voice and started taking her to concerts. She also appointed teachers for her. Soon nine-year-old Kunjamma was singing at neighbourhood functions. She sang flawlessly, with confidence.

One day, her mother was asked if Kunjamma would record a song. She agreed, and at the age of ten, Kunjamma recorded for the famous HMV music company. With this she became well known under her real name, M.S. Subbulakshmi. Most people referred to her as MSS: M for Madurai, the city she was born in; S for Shanmukhavadivu, her mother's name; and S for her own given name, Subbulakshmi. Over time, MSS was shortened to MS.

In those days, most musicians were not well paid and were supported by wealthy families that patronised art and culture. MS's mother hoped to arrange her marriage to a member of the royal family of Ramanathapuram. MS refused and told her that she did not wish to marry; she wanted to continue to study music.

Her mother then took MS to Madras, where her performance at a festival took everyone by surprise. The sixteen-year-old girl captivated the

Illustrated by Joanna Mendes

audience with her singing—so much so that the organisers got her to perform one more time.

Two years later, MS was given a slot to perform at the December music festival by the prestigious Madras Music Academy.

In Madras, MS met Sadasivam, a freedom fighter and journalist, who offered to manage her career. He promoted her extensively and MS went on to act in a few movies, including the celebrated *Meera*. Sadasivam and she eventually married in 1940.

MS began to focus on her music again. She performed at concerts to raise money for various causes. She was known for her generosity: she donated crores of rupees, not only through benefit concerts, but also from her royalties.

Then MS got interested in something rather more controversial. Until the 1940s, Sanskrit or Telugu songs were sung in the first half of all Carnatic music performances. MS joined the Tamil Isai movement that called for songs to be sung in her mother tongue, Tamil. She was banned from the Music Academy for five years for her support to the cause. But this did not deter her. She began to study Tamil music with even greater earnestness and continued to hold concerts.

In 1966, MS was invited to sing in New York at the United Nations and became the first Indian singer to perform there. She travelled widely, finding new audiences for Carnatic music with her stunning voice that traversed three octaves. She went on to win some of the most prestigious awards in India and was the first musician to be awarded a Bharat Ratna, India's highest civilian award.

MS sang in a number of languages—Sanskrit, Hindi, Bengali, Telugu, Malayalam, Kannada and, of course, Tamil. Her daughter Radha accompanied her and they sang together at concerts for fifty years. MS was a perfectionist and insisted on learning the correct pronunciation of every word she sang and the meaning of every song.

MS led a simple life. She had a small wardrobe with only six saris at any given time. Yet, she was a style icon for many. She was known for her elegant Kanchipuram saris and her iconic Blue Jager diamond nose ring. A weaver once made a sari for her in a vibrant shade of blue—MS often wore it on stage. The colour came to be known as MS Blue.

MS died at the age of eighty-eight, after having enthralled audiences in India and around the world for seven decades.

• •

·INDIRA PRIYADARSHINI· GANDHI

Woman in Command

Indira was very excited. She was standing with her family on the terrace of their house, Anand Bhavan, in Allahabad. There was a pile of 'foreign' clothes in front of her—burnt to ashes.

Indira's parents, the Nehrus, were at the forefront of India's struggle for independence. One day, Indira asked Gandhiji how she could get involved in the freedom movement, and he suggested that she form a children's khadi-spinning group. Indira did exactly that and the group came to be called Bal Charkha Sangh.

Her father, Jawaharlal Nehru, would insist on the family reading together every evening, but he wasn't always home. By the time she turned thirteen, he had been to jail five times and she would visit him there. As a result, her school life was disrupted. She learnt to be independent, surrounding herself with books and nature.

Indira's mother, Kamala, didn't want her to be shackled by 'girls' clothes' and often dressed her in kurtas, so Indira was sometimes mistaken for a little boy.

Once, Indira saw a group of students hoisting the Indian flag. When the police lathi-charged them, the leader of the group handed the flag to Indira and told her, 'Don't let it fall'. Although Indira fell and got hurt during the procession, she kept the flag aloft. That's how determined she was even at a young age.

When Indira finished school at sixteen, she received a telegram from her father: 'Going to other home'. He was off to jail again. Shortly afterwards, Indira left to study at Santiniketan, although it wouldn't be for long. It

Illustrated by Ayesha Broacha

was decided that her mother, who was frequently ill, would move to Switzerland for treatment, and Indira would accompany her. Sadly, her mother died soon after Indira turned eighteen, after which she went to study at Oxford.

Once, at a public gathering near Oxford, Indira was asked to speak unprepared. She was too flustered to say anything and heard a man comment, 'She doesn't speak, she squeaks!' Everyone laughed and Indira vowed never to speak in public again.

But she was soon to break her vow. While travelling in South Africa, she was so moved by the appalling living conditions of the railway workers that she took the microphone at a reception and spoke passionately about their plight. This was reported in the papers the following day, and she found herself in the spotlight. Women kissed her hand wherever she went.

In 1942, Indira married Feroze Gandhi and had two sons. After India became independent, with Nehru as its first prime minister, she served as her father's unofficial personal assistant. A few years later, she joined the Congress Party. She was the minister for information and broadcasting in Prime Minister Lal Bahadur Shastri's cabinet when he died. There was a great deal of suspense about who would succeed him. Finally, it was Indira who was chosen to lead the Congress Party and she became India's first woman prime minister. Many thought she was a powerless figurehead, but she proved them wrong. She took and held decisive positions and defied party leaders along the way.

In 1971, Indira Gandhi supported East Pakistan as it strove to be an independent nation. India provided shelter, food and medicines for thousands of East Pakistani refugees fleeing violence at home. The Indian Army, under a joint command with Bangladeshi forces, fought and defeated the Pakistan Army. This was one of Indira's finest moments as a leader.

However, in 1975, India experienced one of its darkest moments under Indira. For fear of losing control over her government and in the face of stiff opposition led by Jayaprakash Narayan, she declared an Emergency. She suspended the Constitution, censored the Indian media, expelled all foreign media, and arrested Opposition leaders. Her son Sanjay carried out a forced sterilisation programme. All this went against the democratic ideals that the country was built on. Seemingly unaware of public opinion, she called for elections—in which she was voted out of office. Four years later, though, she was re-elected.

Indira spearheaded the tiger conservation programme, allocating land for national parks and supporting laws for the protection of endangered animals. She also promoted indigenous crafts and was known to wear only handloom or khadi cotton and silk saris.

During the 1980s there was an insurgency in Punjab, with radical Sikh militants demanding independence for the state. In 1984, they occupied the Golden Temple in Amritsar, whereupon Indira ordered the Indian Army to enter the complex and root them out. Operation Bluestar led to over a thousand deaths. The temple was riddled with bullet holes. The Sikhs were furious: the prime minister had reduced their holiest place of worship to a scene of bloodshed and violence. Not only that, in the days that followed, political leaders and young men were arrested and detained across the state.

Six months later, on the morning of 31 October, Indira Gandhi was assassinated by her own bodyguards, members of the Sikh community. More than twenty bullets were pumped into her body. She was taken to the hospital and was declared dead several hours later.

Indira's last speech was prescient. She said, 'I do not worry if I live or not. As long as there is any breath in me, I shall continue serving you. When I die, every single drop of my blood will give strength to India and sustain a united India.'

Heads of state and leaders from around the world arrived to attend Indira's funeral at Shakti Sthal. The next few days, however, were horrific as thousands of Sikhs were killed in Delhi and elsewhere.

While Indira Gandhi is rightly remembered for her strength and leadership, the consequences of some of her decisions have resulted in a conflicted legacy.

• •

Illustrated by Alia Sinha

·MAHASWETA DEVI·

Writer–Activist

Khuku stared in shock at her brother and sister as they barged into the house from the street. They were covered in black from head to toe and were giggling hysterically. 'But Didi,' they yelled, 'it was so much fun to go and sit in the tar bucket.' They whined as she dragged them off to the bathroom to clean up with hot water and soap. She was determined to get every little spot out and scrubbed so hard that they screamed!

As the eldest, Khuku was more like a little mother to her eight siblings. Because she felt that she was in charge, she could be quite strict. But when the children were ready to go to bed, Khuku would make up the most exciting stories to tell them.

Khuku's father was a poet and her mother a reader. They had a large library with thousands of books. Khuku was always reading. They were often visited by prominent writers and poets—she even met Pearl S. Buck when the eminent novelist was in Calcutta!

As a young adult, Khuku decided to become a teacher. That's when people started to call her by her real name—Mahasweta. Mahasweta was a powerful storyteller. Her fantastic horror stories would have everyone listening to her with rapt attention. She loved seeing the fear on their faces.

Later in her life, Mahasweta was inspired by the story of Rani Lakshmibai. She headed to Jhansi to learn more about her. Back home, she wrote her first book in Bengali—*Jhansir Rani*. Her writing was just like her speech—clear and straightforward.

Soon afterwards, she started to spend more and more time in the villages, especially with the Sabar tribe. The Sabars are poor people who live in forests in houses made of twigs and mud. They survive on food from the forest, including berries, roots, plants, insects, turtles, rabbits and snakes.

When the British ruled India, they thought all Sabars were thieves. They labelled them as criminal tribes. This meant that everyone in the tribe had to register with the police—even if they had never done anything wrong. They were treated badly and often beaten up for no fault of theirs.

Not much changed when the British left, for the Sabars continued to be bullied by the police and other people. This angered Mahasweta greatly. Having spent time with them, she understood the hardships that the tribal people faced every day. She worked hard to get the Indian government to remove the 'criminal' tag, but no action was taken. She then worked with a community of schools called Sabar Samiti, teaching children in tribal villages. She stayed in these villages for months. She was greatly loved and was called Ma by most people. During this time she wrote two award-winning novels based on what she saw and experienced first-hand. While these were widely appreciated, very little was done to improve the lives of the tribals.

Mahasweta wrote many fun books for children, including *The Why-Why Girl*, which was about a girl from the Sabar community, and *Our Incredible Cow*. This was based on a non-vegetarian, alcohol-drinking cow called Nyadosh that would come into her house, climb up the stairs and look at the moon. A strange cow indeed!

Mahasweta wrote more than a hundred books, including plays, novels and short stories. Some of her books were made into movies. Later in life, illness prevented her from travelling to the villages. She died in 2016, when she was ninety years old, but her books and her work with—and for—tribal people will be remembered forever.

• •

·LATA MANGESHKAR·
& ASHA BHOSLE

The Mangeshkar Sisters

Lata, Asha, Usha, Meena and their brother Hridyanath grew up in a house in Sangli, Maharashtra. Their father, Dinanath Mangeshkar, was a well-known classical singer and an actor who also ran a theatre company. The Sangli household teemed with relatives, friends and hordes of children. The children would entertain themselves with all sorts of games, from rolling car tyres down the street to making up plays and enacting them. Lata was always the hero and Meena the villain, while Asha played the princess.

When Lata was about five years old, her father was teaching a raga to a young boy. At some point, he left the room to attend to something, and the student continued to sing. Lata listened for a while, then went inside and told him, 'That's not right. This is how it must be sung.' She proceeded to show him how.

The next day, her father handed Lata a tanpura and started teaching her music. Lata didn't enjoy the lessons very much and usually made excuses to avoid them. She would pretend she had a stomach ache or a headache and run out of the room. When her father confronted her one day, she admitted, 'Baba, I am scared to sing in front of you.'

'I am your father, but also your guru. A good student must always be better than her guru. Never feel shy singing in front of me,' was his response.

Lata's father struggled to make ends meet. His theatre company was constantly in debt. After some years, he sold their house and moved to Pune. Lata performed at a few concerts with her father, but he passed away when she was only thirteen. As the oldest sibling, she had to work

Illustrated by Teju Jhaveri

to provide for the family. She acted in minor roles in a few Marathi films. But she did not like the glare of the studio lights and the camera, and being ordered around by others.

When the family finally moved to Bombay, her mentor, Master Vinayak, took her to Bombay Talkies to record a song. That was a turning point. Lata soon started singing for many composers. She would run from studio to studio recording songs; sometimes she would record six songs in a day without having anything to eat because she did not know that film studios had canteens.

In 1947, Lata was introduced to the actor Dilip Kumar. She was taken aback when he joked that Maharashtrians could never sing in Urdu because their songs smelled of daal-bhaat. Lata was furious and took it upon herself to engage a teacher and master Urdu. In the course of her long career, she recorded songs in thirty-six Indian and foreign languages.

Before she sang, Lata would take off her sandals—her father used to say that singing was like praying in a temple. Even at a performance at the Royal Albert Hall in cold London, she removed her footwear and stood on stage for hours.

All those who have sung with Lata hold her in high esteem. Manna Dey, himself a famous singer, said he had to improve his singing when recording with her because she had an almost perfect voice.

Lata has received several national and international awards. After winning at the Filmfare Awards many times in a row, in the early 1970s, she decided that she would no longer accept one. She thought this would give younger singers a chance to be recognised.

Lata's younger sister, Asha, had a different beginning to her musical career. She got married early, when she was only sixteen. Lata felt that she was too young to marry, and the sisters stopped speaking to each other for a while. In the end, Asha's marriage did not last. She came back to her mother's house, pregnant and with two children in tow.

That was when Asha began singing for films, like her older sister. She struggled to start with, as she was up against many established singers. She sang for low-budget films for years and was paid very little money. Despite being the star of the playback singing circuit, Lata did little to help her at this time.

Asha's career took off when she sang for the young composer R.D. Burman, also called Pancham. His westernised tunes broke the mould of conventional film music. It was through these songs that people began to notice the amazing singer with a playful lilt to her voice.

Pancham admired Asha and sent her flowers for years without his name on the accompanying card. One day, he was around when she received a bouquet of roses. Asha asked for the flowers to be thrown away. 'Some fool keeps sending me roses,' she said. A common friend, who was present, laughed. He told Asha that the fool was none other than the dejected looking Pancham. The two eventually married.

Many thought Asha could sing only 'pop' songs, but she proved them wrong. Her ghazals for the movie *Umrao Jaan* won her great acclaim as well as awards. In 1996, she became the first Indian singer to be nominated for a Grammy Award.

Sadly, Asha suffered great personal losses all through her life. Pancham died after fourteen years of marriage. In 2012, Asha's daughter, who was said to be depressed, shot herself. A few years later, her elder son died of cancer.

Asha carries on. Her cooking is famous in her social circles, and she is now a partner in a chain of Indian restaurants in the Middle East. She has taught the chefs who work there some of her special recipes.

The Mangeshkar sisters have sung an extraordinary number of songs. Most of the young singers we see on television shows today are reprising old songs first sung by Lata or Asha. And thus they remain a part of so many people's lives.

• •

Illustrated by Priya Kuriyan

·LEILA SETH·

A Just Life

Leila was sitting in the darkness, watching the fireflies around her. Paksi—the town in which she and her family lived—had no electricity at that time of the night. Leila was very excited. Her father, who was in the railways, was going to take her and her siblings with him for an important job—an inspection of the railway tracks! Leila loved sitting in the open trolley that was pushed along the rail to check the tracks.

One day, while her father was at work, a man came to their house with some presents. Her mother refused to take them, but the man insisted that she keep at least two flower vases. When her father came home, he was upset with his wife and said that the present was a 'bribe'—something given in return for a favour. When Leila's mother wondered how such an inexpensive gift could be a bribe, he told her that 'on a grey or black sheet, many marks may go unobserved; on a white sheet, even a speck of grey will show'. Leila would never forget his words.

Years later, when Leila was about twenty, she married a young man named Prem Seth. Shortly after they had their first child, the couple moved to London. Prem encouraged Leila to study further, but she had to find something that required the least attendance so she could care for their son too. That is how she decided to study law.

In 1957, 508 students appeared for the Bar exam. Only 152 passed and ten got a distinction; three of them were women. The one who topped was a twenty-eight-year-old married woman with two children (she'd just had another child) called Leila Seth.

When Leila and her family moved back to India, she started practicing law. Initially, people were sceptical—women lawyers were rare at the time. One client even addressed her as Leila Babu, as though she were a man. Her peers gossiped about her, calling her frivolous, convinced that she would not be able to do a good job. Only the older lawyers, to whom she posed no threat, were helpful.

Leila proved her mettle and handled many different kinds of cases at the Patna High Court for a decade, before moving to the Delhi High Court. Seven years later, the Supreme Court named her senior advocate.

A year after that, Leila Seth became the first woman judge in the Delhi High Court. For the first few years, lawyers addressed her as 'My Lord' instead of 'My Lady' because they just weren't used to a woman judge!

Leila's career continued to soar and, in 1991, she became Chief Justice of the Himachal Pradesh High Court, the first woman in the country to hold such a position. She retired shortly afterwards.

Post retirement, Justice Seth was appointed to various commissions and committees. Among them was one that recommended amendments to the Hindu Succession Act, so that daughters could get equal rights to familial property. She was also part of the Justice Verma Committee that changed the definition of rape. All her life, she was a vocal proponent of women's rights and gay rights.

Leila Seth passed away at the age of eighty-six from a cardiac arrest. Even in her death, she helped others by donating her body for organs and medical research.

·KISHORI AMONKAR·

Perfectionist

Kishori came back from school with her brother and sister. While they went out to play, she quietly got out her tanpura and started her riyaaz. Her mother, Mogubai Kurdikar, was her teacher, and Kishori was one of her many students. Kishori understood even at a young age that to be really good she needed to practise regularly.

Kishori used to accompany her mother and the other students to temples and small functions to sing. She found that most people treated women singers poorly. They had to travel third-class on trains and were made to stay in out-of-the-way places. People often spoke disrespectfully to them.

As she grew older, Kishori started singing alone. One day, she recorded a song for a film. When she came back and excitedly told her mother about it, she was asked, 'Are you going to sing for films now?' Kishori replied, 'Yes, everyone liked what I did and I see a bright future for myself.' Her mother said to her, 'If that is your choice, do not touch my tanpuras ever again.'

Kishori was shocked and immediately abandoned all thoughts of singing for films. She went right back to her Hindustani music and soon became a well-known singer.

One day, a woman walked out to get paan in the middle of her performance. Kishori stopped the concert and refused to sing for an audience that didn't respect her music. She told the organisers that they had to learn to treat women as artistes, not just entertainers.

At the peak of her career, Kishori lost her voice. She told herself that God wanted her to stop singing and plunged into the study of music instead. She read ancient texts on musicology. Her friend, Vibha Purandare,

Illustrated by Girija Hariharan

visited her practically every day. Kishori would whisper to her, speaking of the mystery of music and its structures, and Vibha would take notes.

Kishori emerged from her silence a few years later, a different singer altogether. Her music was rooted in the Jaipur–Atrauli gharana, which had a mathematical structure to its rhythm. Her immersion in the theory of music allowed her to push boundaries, to reach the edge of a piece and expand it. Her unique embellishments of existing musical forms made people speak of a new Kishori Amonkar gharana.

Kishori believed that the language of music should be infused with feeling. When she performed at a concert, her audience was God and she was offering an aradhana to Him through the ragas she sang.

Since Kishori travelled frequently for concerts, her children were brought up by her sister and mother for the most part. But she was usually home for Diwali, and would spend four days making a rangoli based on the paintings of Raja Ravi Varma. She would also cook for the children when she was home. Her son said to her once, 'Mummy, even your vegetables are cut to such perfection that if you took a vernier caliper and measured them, they would all be equal.'

One day, Kishori woke up early as usual and started to practise, although she wasn't feeling well. Her son knew she had a concert that evening but didn't see why she needed to push herself so hard. He said, 'Mummy, you have sung all your life. Even if I wake you in the middle of the night, you will sing perfectly.' She replied, 'Just like you have to eat to live, you have to practise to sing well. You will never be perfect, no matter what.'

Kishori spent ten years writing a book on the theory of music. At the age of eighty-four, she died in her sleep. Not only was she a brilliant exponent of her chosen form of music, but she also nurtured the talent of several younger musicians who keep her legacy alive.

• •

Illustrated by Priyanka Tampi

·ELA R. BHATT·

In Sewa

Ela was born in 1933, when India was in the throes of the freedom struggle. Ela's family was also part of the movement. As a child, she and her two sisters saw several of their family members going to jail. There were many conversations in their home about Gandhiji and freedom. Shy, serious Ela would sit quietly and listen to all the adults talk.

When Ela was nine years old, a policeman entered their home to do a surprise check for anything that could be construed as anti-British. As he went towards the pooja room, Ela, who knew there was a banned book there, stopped him and said that he could not enter the room as he had not had a bath. He left.

One summer, Ela and her cousins got together and crept into their neighbour's mango orchard to play. They plucked three raw mangoes, went back home and made a little salad for lunch. When the family sat down to eat, Ela's aunt asked where the mangoes had come from. The neighbour's garden, they replied. Ela's father asked them if they had taken permission to pluck the mangoes. When the cousins told him that there had been no one in the orchard except the watchman, he said, 'Did you ask the watchman's permission?' The cousins looked down at their plates and shook their heads. Ela's father was unhappy. 'Do you know that you have committed a theft? You have to take permission before taking something,' he said. He and Ela's mother quietly left the table. Ela realised then that she had done something very wrong.

Many years later, Ela was riding her scooter back from work one day, when a policeman stopped the traffic on her side at a crossing. Not far from her, a couple was pulling a fully loaded hand-cart—they couldn't stop in time because the cart had no brakes. They both fell and were seriously injured. Ela and a few other people helped them up and took them to a hospital. Ela was a qualified lawyer by now and she thought that since the incident had happened when the couple was at work, their employers should pay the hospital bill. But according to the labour laws, as the husband and wife were informal workers, the employers owed them nothing.

Ela went on to study in Israel, where she was inspired by the manner in which the Israeli labour force was organised. They had unions and worked in co-operatives for the most part. In India, on the other hand, 90 per cent of the workers were unorganised and not protected by the law.

Her head brimming with ideas, Ela returned to India and formed a union and then a co-operative bank for poor working women. The union was named SEWA (Self-Employed Women's Association). She wanted to protect women who were not recognised as workers—even those who did simple jobs like milking a cow. The milk went to the market and contributed to the economy, but the woman's effort was not recognised as real work. Ela decided to change that. She wanted informal women workers to get loans from banks, and to be able to avail of healthcare and childcare. She started by providing services to 4000 women. Now SEWA protects 15 lakh women and is growing every day.

Ela lives by the motto 'peed paraayi jaane re'. She wishes children everywhere would learn to be more empathetic and compassionate.

••

· INDIRA JAISING ·

Fearless Feminist

Indira asked her parents, 'Will you be giving a dowry for my wedding?' She had just moved back to Bombay after graduating from college in Bangalore and knew that her parents wanted her to get married. She had recently attended her cousins' weddings—all of them had gone to their new homes with substantial trousseaus consisting of household goods, clothing, jewellery and money.

When her parents replied that it was the norm, Indira knew that the men they were considering for her were not averse to receiving a dowry. She wasn't sure she wanted to spend her life with someone whose ideals were so different from hers, so she refused to get married. She said she wanted to study law. By becoming a lawyer, she thought, she would be able to help other people and actively oppose discrimination against women.

Indira didn't attend many classes in college because she found the lectures uninteresting. Most students would simply read guide books that contained questions and answers from the previous years' examinations. Indira spent time at home instead, reading legal texts from cover to cover. Her lack of attendance got her expelled, but she promptly got admission in another law college and went on to become one of the toppers at the university. She then studied law for a year in England.

Back in Bombay, she joined a law firm and managed to establish a name for herself in the sexist, nepotistic world of law. She finally did marry at the age of thirty-six. Later, she founded The Lawyers' Collective, an advocacy forum for human rights which represented the poor, the dispossessed and the ignored.

In 1984, after the Bhopal gas disaster, Raghu Rai's famous photo of a man burying his young daughter shook the conscience of the world—and

Illustrated by Sheena Deviah

of lawyers like Indira. She, along with many others, fought cases in the Supreme Court on behalf of the victims, seeking appropriate compensation for them.

In 1986, Indira became the first woman to be designated senior advocate by the High Court of Bombay. She fought and won ground-breaking cases involving the rights of women, including equal inheritance rights for Syrian-Christian women and the right of Hindu mothers to be the natural guardians of minor children. In 2009, she became the first woman to be appointed Additional Solicitor General.

Many years later, Indira took up the case of a student group called Happy to Bleed. The young women were challenging the ban that prevented women of menstruating age from entering the Sabarimala temple. Indira's own experience as a child triggered an emotional connection to the case. When she had just started menstruating, she had absolutely no idea what do. She belonged to a large, conservative Sindhi joint family, and although there were many women around her, no one at home or school had ever spoken to her of puberty. She didn't know what menstruation was or why it had happened to her. Her mother just handed her a pack of sanitary napkins and told her how to use them. And that was it.

In August 2017, Indira Jaising did a 'gown wapasi'. She argued in court that senior advocates should not dress differently or put their title in front of their name. 'One bar, one gown' is what she wanted. In solidarity with junior advocates, she returned her 'senior gown'. Many of her peers openly admired her, but none followed suit.

Indira has also been arguing for live streaming of important cases. She believes this will help students, parliamentarians and others to understand how judgements are made and also compel lawyers to behave better in court.

• •

Illustrated by Priyanka Paul

·ARUNA ROY·

Right to Information

Four-year-old Aruna had her nose deep in a book. She loved to escape into the worlds hidden between the covers of storybooks. At night she had dreams in which she traipsed through enchanted forests, made friends with mysterious creatures, and was chased by giants and witches. Despite the scary dreams, the next day she read more stories!

Aruna loved her parents, but they did not always agree with her. This upset her greatly. Her mother would say, 'Don't cry, Aruna. Argue and tell us why you do not like what we are saying.' Her father taught her to analyse and discuss her problems. Her mother wanted her children to read widely. She told Aruna stories of the scientists Galileo and Ramunajam, and of the Buddha, Christ and Mohammad. She told her tales from the Panchatantra and the Odyssey. Almost every festival was celebrated in their home, so Aruna and her siblings grew up unafraid of people who were 'different'.

When Aruna finished college, she qualified as an Indian Administrative Services (IAS) officer. In the 1960s, very few women were working professionals. Although Aruna worked hard, she was very disappointed with the way things were. She felt many of the officers did not work according to the law and did little for the poor.

Aruna didn't like calling her seniors 'sir', nor did she like being called 'madam' by people much older than her. She often felt that the system was like a spider's web. The more she struggled, the more trapped she felt—and this was no childhood nightmare. Finally, despite much opposition from her family and friends, Aruna left the IAS. She joined her husband, Bunker Roy, who had set up an organisation dedicated to understanding the problems of rural life in Rajasthan.

In 1987, she set up a people's organisation, Mazdoor Kisan Shakti Sangathan (MKSS), with activists Shankar Singh, Nikhil Dey and a few others.

The situation was dire. They could see that workers in Rajasthan were being cheated of their rightful wages. Corrupt panchayats and officials would bill the government large amounts but pay the workers very little. People had no access to their own records.

When Aruna and her colleagues at MKSS asked the panchayats for their lists of workers, as well as bills and vouchers, their request was denied. Under the Official Secrets Act, no information could be given. That was when they began to campaign for the right to information.

Activists sat on a forty-day dharna and hunger strike in the town of Beawar. People from over 150 villages participated, including many women with babies on their laps. More than 400 people protested every day. The villagers donated food, water and whatever little money they could to keep the protests going. The media took note and started to report on the agitation.

Eventually, the Right to Information (RTI) Act was passed in Parliament in 2005. Aruna says, 'Now we can ask anyone in government to tell us why teachers do not come to school, why we don't have playgrounds, why people don't get paid what they are promised, why buses do not run properly.'

The RTI Act gives people the right to find out what is happening in their name. You can now file an application for information online. As long as there is injustice and the poor continue to suffer, Aruna says she will continue her battle.

● ●

·J. JAYALALITHAA·

Ammu to Amma

Ammu was sad. Her teachers had praised an essay that she had written on her mother. However, Ammu had not been able to share this happy news with her mother, who was an actor in Tamil films and had not come home for two days. When her mother finally tiptoed in, she found Ammu fast asleep, a notebook on her lap. As she removed the book, Ammu woke up and read out the essay. Her mother was delighted. She promised Ammu she would spend more time at home. But she couldn't keep that promise.

Ammu hated the film industry that kept her mother away from her. She decided that when she grew up she would become an IAS officer or a doctor or a lawyer.

Over the years, Ammu learnt Bharatanatyam, classical piano and Carnatic music. Sometimes she would accompany her mother to the film sets. Once, a Kannada film producer saw beautiful Ammu, a teenager now, and asked her to act in his film. Ammu had a two-month holiday before starting college. She decided she would do the film to keep herself busy. With that decision, Komalavalli (Ammu's real name) faded away and Jayalalithaa entered the movies.

The film offers kept coming and Jayalalithaa could not say no. Her father had died when she was a young girl and the family had little money. Her earnings would keep them going. Despite her negative feelings about the industry, Jayalalithaa braced herself and entered the world of films.

In the next twenty years, Jayalalithaa acted in over one hundred Kannada, Tamil and Telugu movies, many opposite male actors twice her age. One of them was M.G. Ramachandran, an actor who went on to found the political party, AIADMK (All-India Dravida Munnetra Kazhagam).

Illustrated by Priyanka Tampi

Jayalalithaa joined the AIADMK with MGR's encouragement. Her oratorial skills were extraordinary. Her speeches were lauded and she swiftly rose through the party ranks. In 1987, MGR died and Jayalalithaa became the head of the party. She was now the leader of the Opposition in Tamil Nadu, which was ruled by the DMK (Dravida Munnetra Kazhagam).

The chief minister, M. Karunanidhi, was worried about Jayalalithaa's popularity and dynamism. One day, the conflict between the two parties came to a head in the legislative assembly. Jayalalithaa and her party members interrupted the chief minister's speech and accused him of being corrupt. The house was in chaos. Chappals were thrown, papers were torn up, but the most shocking act of all was committed by a male member of the DMK, who pulled at Jayalalithaa's sari pallu. Furious, she said she would not enter the house again until the dignity of women was restored.

Soon after this, Jayalalithaa defeated Karunanidhi in the elections and became the chief minister of Tamil Nadu. Over the next twenty-five years, either the AIADMK or the DMK was in power, with Jayalalithaa being elected chief minister four times.

In her first term as chief minister, Jayalalithaa started the Cradle Baby Scheme. Newborn girls were being killed in alarming numbers in rural Tamil Nadu at the time. Now, poor mothers could leave their baby daughters in cradles in villages and towns. The children would be sent for adoption or supported by the government. Over 3600 babies were saved by this scheme.

Once, at a party meeting, Jayalalithaa met Sasikala Natarajan, a videographer and the wife of a government official. Over the years she became Jayalalithaa's closest confidante. People say that Sasikala influenced Jayalalithaa negatively and open corruption became the norm in the AIADMK. Jayalalithaa seemed to turn a blind eye to all that was going on. To make matters worse, she adopted Sasikala's nephew. She arranged a lavish public wedding for him, spending hundreds of crores of rupees. It was splashed across the media and people were shocked and angry with her. Even members of her own party were unhappy. She was voted out of power in the next election. Her home was raided by law enforcement agencies. Gold, money, jewellery, shoes, land documents, investment portfolios and luxury cars were confiscated.

A case of corruption was filed against her and she was arrested and sent to jail. She came out on bail and made a public statement accusing Karunanidhi of conspiring to put her behind bars. The court finally acquitted her.

In her third term as chief minister, Jayalalithaa introduced more schemes for the welfare of the poor, especially women. People started to call her Amma—mother.

Jayalalithaa found that girls dropped out of school after they started menstruating, so she introduced a scheme to provide sanitary napkins for young girls in school. She also supported the education of women and provided bicycles for young girls so they could get to their schools. Every woman from a poor family who finished a college degree received some gold and cash from the government.

She introduced the popular Amma Canteens that served breakfast and lunch at low prices for the poor. She was also responsible for the introduction of the first force of women commandos in Tamil Nadu.

But the past came back to haunt her. Jayalalithaa had more money than she could have earned through honest means, and several corruption cases had been instituted against her. These dragged on for two decades. Finally, a lower court in Karnataka convicted her and she was asked to pay a fine and sentenced to four years in jail. But soon afterwards, the Karnataka High Court acquitted her.

Chief Minister Jayalalithaa fell seriously ill in 2016 and was taken to hospital. She remained there for over two months before she died.

Jayalalithaa's legacy is gravely conflicted. On the one hand, she was a formidable leader who brought in much-needed administrative reforms and focused on women's issues, but on the other, she was every bit the corrupt politician.

• •

Illustrated by Sujata Bansal

·SUDHA VARGHESE·

Leading the Band

Chinnamma, or Sudha, was the oldest child in a family of eight and very close to her parents. Her father was a landowner in Kottayam, who farmed alongside the Dalit workers who came to work in the fields with their children. Chinnamma happily played in the fields and ate her meals with the other children. Her parents had never told her to treat the workers differently, although she knew from their clothing that they were poor.

At sixteen, Sudha happened to meet some nuns from the religious order Notre Dame. She found them extremely kind and helpful, and decided that she would join them.

After studying with the nuns for a few years, Sudha was sent to work in Patna, where people from the Musahar community lived. The Musahars were among the poorest Dalits in the country and suffered extremely harsh conditions. During her seven years there, Sudha realised that most Dalits were not even aware of their rights.

The Musahars were exploited in many ways. The 'upper castes' did not allow them to repair their own huts, or to keep chairs and charpoys inside their homes. From time to time, 'upper-caste' men would enter their villages and rape the women. Musahars were beaten if they went near the temples—the same temples they had helped build. Such inhuman behaviour was a way of life.

Sudha left the order of the nuns and stayed on in Bihar. She was determined to make a difference. She went to study law in Bangalore, and on her return to Patna, set up Nari Gunjan, an NGO that focused on education for women, vocational training and jobs, and provided assistance to victims of violence.

Sudha came up with the novel idea of empowering women through music. She gathered twelve young women and hired a teacher who taught them to play the drums. Initially, this caused a lot of hullabaloo in the village—a band of women drummers was unheard of! But Sudha and the women were determined. Gradually news about them spread. A man who had seen them on TV called Sudha, asking if the band would play at his wedding. Since then, they have been called upon several times, especially during the wedding season. The women now earn a daily wage higher than their husbands and travel all over Bihar. More importantly, they feel respected.

Sudha set up a girls' school and hostel with the help of the Bihar government to educate young girls from the Musahar community. She also runs a small orphanage about two kilometres from the hostel and cycles there every day to spend time with the children. She holds summer camps for young girls to teach them self-defence, writing, acting, cooking and oratory.

Sudha has spent over forty years in Patna and continues to work tirelessly for the community. Inspired by Dr B.R. Ambedkar and his fight against untouchability, she believes that no woman should ever give up. No matter how difficult the obstacles, you can overcome them if you set your mind to it.

• •

· RASHIDA BI & ·
CHAMPA DEVI SHUKLA

Accidental Activists

Champa grew up in a small town near Jabalpur. Her father had just bought a house that was formerly a small police station. Every day, as she walked back from school, she would look forward to playing cops and robbers and locking up 'thieves' (her siblings) in the cells.

At the age of thirteen, Champa got married.

In another town near Bhopal, ten-year-old Rashida was sitting inside her house, wishing she could go out and play with the neighbourhood children. There was a lake nearby and she could hear their happy shrieks as they jumped into the water. But Rashida was not allowed to go out of her house; neither could she attend school. From 7 a.m. to 11 p.m., she and her siblings rolled beedis. The family was paid Rs 2 for 1,000 beedis. It was not an easy life. Her parents were constantly worried about getting her married. Finally, at age thirteen, she was married to a tailor in Bhopal.

Rashida's new family had very little money. Her mother had always warned her that marriage was like chickpeas made of iron (*lohe ke chane*)—difficult to eat and digest, but unavoidable. So when Rashida went for days without food in her married home, she thought it was normal. She didn't even have soap to bathe or wash her clothes.

Meanwhile, Champa's husband, who worked for the Indian Railways, kept getting transferred around the country. When they finally moved to Bhopal, they stayed in a colony not far from Rashida's house.

Both women's homes were close to a large factory that manufactured pesticides—the Union Carbide factory.

Illustrated by Aparajita Ninan

On the night of 2 December 1984, twenty-one-year-old Rashida and her family woke up gasping for air. Her nephew wondered if someone was burning chillies. Their eyes were stinging; it was hard to find their way around. They could hear screams from outside. Hordes of people were running to the bus stand and the police station. Rashida and her family joined them. Their chests were swollen; they couldn't breathe.

At 4 a.m., an announcement was made that a gas leak at the Union Carbide factory had been contained. Everyone was told to go back home. That was the very first time Rashida heard of Union Carbide.

They couldn't go home—they could barely move. Later that morning, they were taken to a nearby hospital, but the doctors didn't know what to do or how to treat them. Meanwhile, people were dying everywhere. The corridors were full of people who couldn't see or breathe or walk.

Not far away, Champa and her family were also struggling. They had run to the bus stop, hoping to leave the city, but Champa's husband fell on the way, and eventually the whole family collapsed. At the hospital, Champa was devastated to see the number of dead bodies around her.

The poisonous gas leak from the Union Carbide factory killed 2,000 people almost instantly. Over the next few years, it would kill 20,000 and affect over 1,50,000 with illness or deformity.

Both Rashida and Champa had relatives who suffered from blindness, kidney failure, cancer and other diseases. They couldn't work and money was hard to come by. Six months after the tragedy, some neighbours told Rashida about a place where women could sign up to work. For Rs 5 a day, they would make file covers. Only a hundred women were hired; Rashida was one of them. She was scared, but then she saw a kind-looking woman with a big bindi sitting in a corner. It was Champa. Rashida went to sit near her, and soon she and Champa became friends.

The women were not taught any skills, nor given any work. They would sit there for eight hours sharing tragic stories of disease and death.

Three months later, someone told them that they needn't come back the next day. The women were stunned. Their only source of income was gone. The angry women asked Rashida to speak on their behalf to the government—Rashida, who had not stepped out of her home for twenty-one years, who couldn't read or write!

By then Champa and she had become fast friends and they decided to face the challenge together. They walked all the way to the city to meet the chief minister and stood outside his office till he met them. After this, temporary work was allocated to the women for thirty months, at a meagre rate of Rs 3–5 a day.

Soon, Rashida and Champa became the voice of the women victims and survivors. Many senior lawyers argued cases on their behalf for compensation and rehabilitation. The NGO Greenpeace supported them and took them all over the world to talk about the disaster. Union Carbide eventually paid the Government of India a paltry sum of $500 per victim. Very little of this money reached the victims.

Today, Rashida Bi and Champa Devi run an NGO called Chingari. It provides physical and occupational therapy and counselling for second- and third-generation victims of the gas tragedy. Their journey so far has been one of endurance and integrity in the face of impossible odds.

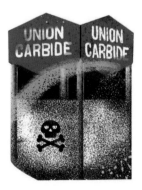

Illustrated by Suhana Medappa

· KIRAN MAZUMDAR-SHAW ·

Entrepreneur for Change

Eleven-year-old Kiran was acting in a play. She and her friends had organised a show with music, dance and drama. The newspapers were full of news of the Sino-Indian war and the children had decided that they wanted to raise money for the brave jawans in the Indian Army. So they had got together, sold tickets to their parents and neighbours and collected money.

The children then went to each shop in the main shopping areas of Bangalore and asked for canned food, blankets, socks—anything that they felt the jawans could use. They packed everything in a large carton and sent it along with a cheque for Rs 200 (the money they had collected from the play tickets) to the then prime minister of India, Jawaharlal Nehru. They were extremely proud of themselves—and of their country.

When she grew up, Kiran decided that she wanted to be a doctor. But the entrance exam was very tough and she missed her chance by just one mark. She went on to study zoology and stood first in her university. She wanted to study further, but she wasn't interested in research and preferred to focus on applied science—'something more practical'. When she asked her father for advice, he suggested that she consider becoming a brewer, like him.

Kiran was appalled. She didn't think the alcohol industry would accept a woman brewer. But her father persuaded her to go to Australia for further studies, and she came back ready to put her new-found knowledge to work. Except, no one in the industry wanted to hire her.

Angry and frustrated at the age of twenty-five, Kiran took a loan from a bank and started a biotechnology company—Biocon—in her garage, in partnership with an Irish company of the same name.

In the late 1990s, Kiran decided to change the focus of her company—to provide life-saving, affordable medicines to people. India had the highest number of patients with diabetes. Insulin, the medicine used to treat the disease, was imported. Most patients simply could not afford it. Kiran thought it was time to stop India's reliance on foreign drugs. She put money into research and Biocon ended up developing insulin at one-tenth the cost of imported insulin. By now, after many years and a tough struggle, Kiran had also managed to free her company from its foreign partners.

One day, a close friend of Kiran's was diagnosed with cancer. Kiran watched helplessly as her friend went from hospital to hospital. Shortly after this, Kiran's husband was found to have cancer too.

In 2000, Kiran started an affordable, state-of-the-art cancer institute in Bangalore, working closely with Dr Devi Shetty, the renowned surgeon. Although cancer was widespread in India, medicines were extremely expensive and some patients were paying almost twenty lakh rupees a year for them. Her scientists developed cancer antibodies and introduced a drug that could treat many types of cancer, especially the one most common among Indian women: breast cancer.

In 2012, dengue and chikungunya were rampant in Bangalore. Mounds of garbage were piling up on the streets and the municipal bodies were doing nothing about it. Kiran, along with some friends, decided it was time for action and together they set up the Bangalore Political Action Group (BPAC).

Today, Kiran is among India's most successful entrepreneurs and business leaders. She is often trolled on social media for taking a stand on issues that she believes in. But she never backs down and always engages with her detractors patiently, yet firmly.

• •

·MEDHA PATKAR·

Constant Crusader

Medha was studying at home, but over the top of her book she was secretly watching her father, a trade union leader. It was Diwali that day. A man had come to the house with a box of sweets. Medha's father gave it one look and threw it out. Medha was shocked because she had been taught that wasting food was wrong. Then she heard her father say angrily to her mother, 'How can we accept anything from a man who did not give his workers a Diwali bonus?' Medha was struck by her father's sense of right and wrong and vowed to be like him.

At school Medha took part in all kinds of activities—elocution, dance, art, writing, debating—and won many medals. Once, a teacher came across one of her notebooks, which was full of poems she had written, and thought they were good enough to be published in the school magazine. But she told Medha that she would use some other students' names too, as it would be strange to put her name under every poem. Medha's poem 'Santra aur Limboo' won a prize, but it went to the girl whose name the teacher had used. When Medha told her mother about this, she was furious and complained to the principal. The following day, at the assembly, the principal announced that it was Medha who had written the winning poem.

Before participating in any debate, Medha would discuss the topic with her father, and he would write down points for her to build on. But when she was twelve, he told her it was time she did her own research and asked her to show him what she planned to say. When she took her notes to him, his response was to throw the piece of paper away. Shocked, Medha asked, 'Why did you do that?' He replied, 'You need to apply yourself far more diligently to sharpen your arguments.'

Her mother told her, 'If you want to convince a person, look into their eyes. Don't look down. People will think you are lying if you look away.' She would get Medha to look in the mirror and practise. Before every

Illustrated by Suhana Medappa

debate, she was trained to speak clearly. This helped her in her future work as well.

In the mid-1980s, the Gujarat government planned a huge project to build over 3000 dams along the Narmada river. Medha, who was around thirty then, joined an NGO called SETU and went to the Narmada Valley to do a survey on the impact the dam would have on the people who lived there.

Medha realised that the dams would wipe out the fertile soil on which the tribal farmers cultivated their crops. They would have to move away from their land, and the government had no plans to provide them with new homes or offer any money for resettlement. Medha walked from village to village to educate the villagers about the risk to their livelihood.

In 1989, Medha formed a group called Narmada Bachao Andolan to resist the building of the dams using non-violent means. She also founded NAPM (National Alliance of People's Movements) to protest injustices against underserved communities through marches, hunger strikes, sit-ins and other methods. Medha has been jailed for her actions many times but she says, 'If you want to make a difference, you should be prepared for both jail and death.'

Medha believes that every school should get its students to spend time in slums and villages. It is only then that a child can truly understand the country's realities and its people.

Illustrated by Ayangbe Mannen

BIRUBALA RABHA

Indomitable Spirit

Birubala's parents had died when she was only six. Living in a remote village in Assam, little Biru kept herself busy. She could raise chickens and roosters, sew and even weave, but she never went to school. At the age of sixteen, she got married to a farmer in Thakurbila. Soon she had a new life and four children.

Her eldest son, Dharmeshwar, suffered from mental health issues. The worried family went to an ojha, a local medicine man, who told them that her son was going to die very soon. The family waited, terrified and heartbroken, but many days went by and nothing happened to Dharmeshwar.

Birubala was furious. She realised that the ojha was taking advantage of the uneducated villagers. When his medicines didn't work, he would blame it on some woman and declare her a 'witch'. Some ojhas declared women witches when they wanted to usurp their property or money. Unmarried women, widows and old couples were often targeted. The people in the village were highly superstitious and believed everything these men said.

Meanwhile, in a neighbouring village, a woman called Sunila was afraid for her life. The local ojha was blaming her for his own inability to cure a young girl of her illness. He said Sunila was a witch and responsible for everything that was going wrong in the village.

When Birubala heard about this, she immediately set out for Sunila's village, walking through the forest for two hours to get there. By the time she reached, Sunila's house was on fire. The villagers were attacking her—pulling her hair, spitting on her and kicking her violently. Birubala ran to Sunila and covered her with a shawl. She screamed at the villagers, 'If Sunila is a witch, why does she bleed like us? Why hasn't she used her powers to get a better house? To become rich? Why does she stay in a mud house like the rest of us?' She then told them her own story—about how an ojha had fooled her family. Slowly the villagers started to walk away and a few helped to take care of Sunila.

Birubala decided she would fight against this superstition and other social evils in her community. She joined a Mahila Samiti in her village.

Once, an ojha in another village held thirty-five women to ransom, declaring them witches. He demanded money from them to hold a 'cleansing' ceremony. If they didn't pay up, they would be cast out of the village. Birubala got the police involved and they managed to rescue the women.

In 2011, Birubala founded Mission Birubala, to provide support to victims of witch-hunting and to help dispel superstitions around the practice. She also petitioned the Assam government to institute a law against witch-hunting. Because of this, she is shunned by many villages in Assam, where people still believe in witches.

In 2015, Birubala Rabha was conferred an honorary doctorate by the University of Guwahati. Meanwhile, her son is being cared for in a professional mental healthcare institution in a nearby town.

·KUMARI MAYAWATI·

Dalit Crusader

Mayawati was travelling on a bus with her mother when someone asked them which caste they belonged to. Her mother answered, 'Chamar.' Immediately, the passengers next to them got up and moved away. A puzzled Mayawati was told by her mother that many people considered Chamars to be unclean.

Every year, on Ambedkar Jayanti, Mayawati would hear speeches about the great leader's life and writings. She asked her father if people would respect her as much as they did Ambedkar if she fought the caste system. He told her that if she became an IAS officer or a collector, she could certainly fight it.

Mayawati studied hard. She did a BA and a B.Ed., and started studying law. Finally, after getting a teaching job at a government school, she began preparing for the UPSC examinations.

Meanwhile, she continued to read Ambedkar's writings and became increasingly aware of the issues the Dalit community faced. She soon got involved with Dalit politics and participated in many political rallies. She came to be known for her passionate oratory.

After hearing about a particularly fervent speech she made when she was twenty-one, on ending the caste system, Kanshi Ram, the leader of BAMCEF (The All India Backward and Minority Communities Employees Federation) went to visit her. He said she was making a mistake by trying to become an IAS officer. There were many IAS officers who were Dalit, but no Dalit leader to get IAS officers to resolve some of the community's problems.

Mayawati soon lost her enthusiasm for the IAS and joined Kanshi Ram and his group. Kanshi Ram was impressed by her dedication. Every day

Illustrated by Rae Zachariah

she would leave early for the school where she taught, then spend the rest of the day working for BAMCEF before attending law college in the evening.

In 1984, the Bahujan Samaj Party (BSP) was formed with Kanshi Ram at the helm and his twenty-eight-year-old mentee Mayawati by his side. Mayawati would go from village to village and speak to people. A young girl in her twenties, she would deliver rousing speeches about the neglect the Dalit community suffered despite being one of the largest groups of voters in the country.

At some point, Kanshi Ram began to focus his attention on other states in north India, pushing Mayawati to the forefront in Uttar Pradesh. In 1995, thirty-nine-year-old Mayawati became India's first woman Dalit chief minister and the youngest ever in UP. She overhauled the administrative system, holding all officers responsible for meeting with the public every day and sending in weekly reports. She increased the representation of Dalits in the government and the judiciary. She funnelled resources to villages with a Scheduled Caste population. Pucca homes, pumps, schools and clinics were built in places with few resources.

Mayawati served as chief minister for three short terms before coming back to power, in 2007, with a resounding majority. She was the first chief minister in Uttar Pradesh to serve a full term of five years. However, she came under fire for her injudicious use of public money. She spent crores of rupees on large statues of Ambedkar, Kanshi Ram and herself in Lucknow. She was also accused of spending large sums on assets and properties, which she claimed were bought with party funds and donations. She lost the next election.

Several politicians—men and women—have attempted to ridicule Mayawati for her appearance and mannerisms. But she remains unfazed. In a feudal state and a bigoted environment, she continues to defy the stereotype of a woman politician—and a Dalit.

• •

Illustrated by Sheena Deviah

·BHANWARI DEVI·

Awaiting Justice

Bhanwari's mother died when she was very young, so Bhanwari had to do all the housework. When she was six, she got married to Mohan, who was from the Kumahar community. At twelve, she moved to her husband's home in Bhateri, a little village in Rajasthan. Her life was much the same there: cooking, cleaning and taking care of the family. When she grew older, she sometimes worked with her husband as a contract labourer.

In 1985, someone from the Government of Rajasthan's Women's Development Programme (WDP) approached Bhanwari and asked if she would become a saathin, a friend of the women. As a saathin, she would help the village women to come together to try and solve their problems. Though Bhanwari was apprehensive, she agreed. They trained her to teach the women in her village about safe conception and childbirth, and to find ways in which they could stand up against violence. She learnt about the importance of education and the need to fight social evils like female foeticide, child marriage and dowry.

The nicest part of it was that, for the first time, Bhanwari made friends. She was now part of a network of saathins from different villages, including the guiding didis who managed the programme. Her training empowered her to start working with the women in Bhateri.

Child marriage was very common in her district. In April 1992, she heard that a nine-month-old baby from a land-owning Gurjar family was to be married. Bhanwari and her supervisor counselled the parents against it, but they refused to listen. Her project director regularly sent reports of all planned marriages to the district collector. These reports eventually reached the police, who had instructions to stop child marriages. That's what happened in Bhanwari's village. The police came to Bhateri and stopped the marriage. However, the ceremony resumed after they left.

The Gurjar family was furious with Bhanwari. How dare she insult them by sending the police to the wedding? They began harassing her. No one was allowed to buy the earthen pots that her family made. She was not allowed to attend any community weddings or poojas. They even beat up her husband Mohan one day. Bhanwari pleaded with them to stop, but they wouldn't listen.

This went on for months.

One day, in September 1992, Bhanwari's calf was refusing to eat any food. So she and Mohan went to the field in the afternoon to harvest some green gram for the calf to feed on. Five men in the neighbouring fields—four of whom belonged to the family of the child bride—saw them, and crossed over to their field. They thrashed Mohan and held him down while two of them raped Bhanwari.

When the men left, Mohan was in despair. He looked at the nearby stream and told Bhanwari that the only way out was suicide. The shame was too much. Bhanwari disagreed. She said, 'I've been telling women to break their silence all this while. Now I have to break my silence.' That was the longest and darkest night of her life. She knew that she would be alone and shunned even more if she complained.

Early in the morning, Bhanwari and Mohan caught a bus and went to Bassi police station to report the incident. A young supervisor from Bhanwari's head office in Jaipur arrived by noon to help and insisted the police file a First Information Report (FIR). The police argued with her for four hours and then grudgingly filed a report. They asked for a medical test, but since there was only a male doctor available, Bhanwari refused. She was then taken to a hospital in Jaipur. But the authorities kept delaying the orders for the test. By the time it was finally done, it was too late to be of any use.

After fifty-two hours of humiliation, an exhausted Bhanwari was brought back to Bassi police station. Here they insulted her further, demanding she give them her ghagra as evidence. With nothing to wear, Bhanwari had to wrap Mohan's thin turban around herself till she could borrow a ghagra from another saathin.

The news of the rape began to spread and several women's rights groups demanded that the Central Bureau of Investigation (CBI) take charge of the case. Activists across the country were outraged, although many politicians and officials refused to believe Bhanwari's story.

Meanwhile, five NGOs, including one called Vishaka, got together to form a group. They filed a Public Interest Litigation (PIL) in the Supreme Court to demand that action be taken against the errant police officers and other officials in the case. Most importantly, they wanted the court to form guidelines for the prevention of harassment of women at work.

Since the CBI in Rajasthan refused to believe Bhanwari, the women activists took her to New Delhi to meet senior officials from the agency. They started a new investigation and, a year later, the case was taken to the courts in Jaipur.

Shockingly, the accused were acquitted of rape in 1995. The presiding judge made statements that had little to do with the law. He said the men who raped Bhanwari were too old. He said Bhanwari had grey hair and she wasn't from the same caste as the men. Why would anyone rape her? Justice Krishna Iyer—a visionary Supreme Court judge—called it a 'black day' for the Indian judiciary.

The case was appealed. In 1996, a judge ruled that the case should follow due process, which meant it would get in line behind the thousands of cases backlogged in the system. It has been over twenty-two years and Bhanwari's appeal has still not come up for hearing.

Bhanwari continues to work in her village. She is now seen as a human rights leader in her district. She helps women, children and men in distress. She earns only Rs 3600 a month as a saathin, but she is committed to the welfare and education of girls and women in her district.

Although Bhanwari has not got justice, a large number of working women in India have benefited from the Vishaka guidelines, which were made into law in 2013. Now, every employer has a responsibility to provide a sexual harassment free workplace. If a woman is harassed, she can file a complaint.

Bhanwari believes she has got some measure of justice from God—three of the men who assaulted her have died. She says, 'Even if I die, continue my fight. Continue the fight for what is right and against all social ills that oppress women.'

• •

·BAMA·

Truth to Power

Six-year-old Faustina stared at the apparatus on the ceiling, going round and round. Her village had got electricity for the first time and she was fascinated by the fan's movement. She was so excited that she ran to the village church to thank God. On the way back, she saw some beautiful hibiscus flowers in a garden that she was not allowed to enter. The garden belonged to someone from an 'upper-caste' home. Faustina crept in, plucked three large blooms and ran home.

She looked around her tiny house, wondering where to place them. Then she saw the three holes of an electrical socket. 'Perfect!' she thought. As she put the first flower in, she got an electric shock. 'Jesus is punishing me,' she thought. 'He knows I have stolen.' She closed her eyes and asked him for forgiveness. Then she put the next flower in and got another shock. She immediately got on her knees and asked Jesus once again to forgive her. A few hours later, the flowers withered and Faustina was even more miserable—God had rejected her offering. She swore to herself that she would never steal again.

One day, Faustina accompanied her grandmother to work. She saw her finish cleaning the house and place a small bowl near the drain outside. The woman of the house appeared, stood as far away from them as possible and tipped some food into the bowl. It was the family's leftover dinner from the night before. Faustina couldn't believe her eyes. Angrily, she asked her grandmother why she was demeaning herself by accepting leftovers. Her grandmother said it had always been that way. They were of a 'lower caste' and had no choice.

Faustina's father was in the army and always told his children that education could bring change. Faustina studied hard and scored the highest marks in her district in Class 10. When her name was called out in the school assembly, her mother's eyes brimmed over with tears.

Illustrated by Tara Anand

Faustina had proved what a Dalit child could do despite having less than half the opportunities that the others did. She decided to study further and become a teacher in order to empower other young Dalit girls.

Faustina thought she would be in a better position to teach others if she became a nun, so she did. But then she discovered that no one was allowed to think creatively or be different in the convent. Even the nuns spoke of and treated Dalits with contempt. After seven years, she left the order, thoroughly disillusioned, without a job or money or support.

It was a difficult time for her. She finally managed to find a job at the Jesuit Social Work Centre. It paid very little. To cope with the misery and confusion she was feeling, she started to write about her life and her experiences.

A friend read what she had written and suggested she get it published. In 1992, the centre she was working at published the book. However, it got poor reviews in the media, and people in her village were furious with her for writing about them and the church in such a negative way. They didn't let her enter her village for seven months.

But her friends from the centre continued to encourage Faustina. They felt her writing was a powerful way of highlighting caste and gender barriers in society. *Karukku* was eventually translated into English and many other languages and became a bestseller. It was one of the first autobiographies to be written by a Tamil Dalit woman and is today in its twenty-fifth year of publication.

Faustina went on to write more books using the pen name Bama. She taught in a primary school in rural Tamil Nadu for 22 years before retiring.

Illustrated by Aarti Malik

104

·SUNITA NARAIN·

Green Campaigner

Sunita was sitting in the back of an Ambassador car, curled up on the seat. The floor of the car was full of plants—and seven people were squeezed in too.

Sunita's father had passed away when she was eight, and her mother had brought up four daughters single-handedly. Every holiday, she and the girls, along with a friend and her son, would drive to a hill station. When they drove back home, the car would be full of saplings. Sunita's mother managed to grow some unique plants in their Delhi garden—chinar, apple, olive, even a gingko grew under her green thumb! None of the girls was allowed to pluck a single leaf from the garden.

Sunita was fascinated by all aspects of nature. When she was fifteen, she met two young students at an environment conference who shared her passion. From then on, they met every Sunday to explore the Delhi Ridge and study its plants. They went on to join a group called Kalpavriksh, an organisation that works on environmental and social issues.

When Sunita finished school, she wanted to work for the environment. But no one knew what that meant. People thought she wanted to study the weather. Finally, through a family friend, she met a man named Kartikeya Sarabhai, who ran an environmental research organisation in Ahmedabad. Sunita spent a year there learning about the Gir forest.

Back in Delhi, she met Anil Agarwal, who wanted to create a State of India environment report. Sunita was twenty years old when she joined his organisation, the Centre for Science and Environment (CSE).

In 1996, Delhi was covered by a blanket of smog. The CSE team and Sunita led a campaign to clean up the air in the city. They went to court to get all public transport to switch from pollution-causing diesel to compressed natural gas (CNG). A few years later, despite huge resistance, the court passed the order which helped reduce air pollution in Delhi.

Sunita and her team were also concerned about food safety. They tested some aerated drinks and found poisonous pesticide residues above the permissible limit in them. A battle began against the giant cola companies, which claimed that Sunita's allegations were false. But her stand was clear: India was too poor to undertake a clean-up programme after having its people poisoned. She wanted the companies to set higher standards.

Sunita believes everyone has the right to clean air and water and everyone can, and should, help improve the conditions of our planet. What she does not like is the lazy and cynical attitude of people who say, 'Chalta hai'.

• •

·GAURI LANKESH·

A Gutsy Life

Gauri was running a race in school. All the other girls were ahead of her. Gauri hated sports, but the school had insisted that she take part in the race. She came in last and went home dejected. Her father, however, felt she deserved a prize for participation and gave her a book. Gauri was delighted.

Lankesh, her father, ran a popular Kannada newspaper called *Lankesh Patrike*, which regularly published investigative stories. It was the only newspaper in India in those days that relied entirely on subscriptions, instead of earning money through advertisements.

When Gauri grew older, her father would occasionally give her a blank cheque with no amount on it, just his signature. She and her younger siblings would go to their favourite bookstore armed with the cheque. Many years later, she still remembered it as a fantastic adventure!

Gauri's mother wanted her to become an engineer or a doctor, but she wanted to be a writer, like her father. Her mother then told her that she should at least marry a doctor. And so a match was arranged.

On hearing that a boy was coming to meet her, Gauri was deeply upset. She stomped off to a salon, where she got them to chop off her beautiful tresses and came back home sporting a 'boy cut'. Her family was aghast and gave her a really hard time, but she refused to fall in line.

Gauri went on to marry a dear friend whom she loved, and they moved to Delhi. One day, she received news that her father had died. Her brother, who ran the sports section of *Lankesh Patrike*, asked Gauri to return to Bangalore and edit the paper, as he knew very little about politics. To keep the legacy of her father alive, she agreed.

Illustrated by Shruti Prabhu

Her first big challenge was writing, and editing, in Kannada. She worked hard at it and did so well that within a year, she was correcting other people's proofs.

Gauri reported often on the failures of the government and also wrote in support of Naxal ideology—something her brother did not agree with. This finally led to her starting her own newspaper, *Gauri Lankesh Patrike*.

Gauri was an atheist who believed in communal harmony. She and her siblings had a tradition of celebrating various religious festivals. Her sister organised the celebrations for Christmas, her brother for different Hindu festivals, and Gauri celebrated Bakrid. They would get together and spend hours discussing politics.

On 5 September 2017, Gauri was tragically shot and killed by three men. While the reason for the murder has not been established, many believe that it was a violent reaction to her assertive journalism.

Gauri enjoyed the company of young people and had 'adopted' a number of young activists. In 2018, on her birth anniversary, these young men and women came together with other activists, writers and journalists across India to celebrate Gauri Day.

• •

Illustrated by Sayalee Karkare

·KALPANA CHAWLA·

Space Woman

'What's her name?' the primary school principal asked Mantoo's older sister. It was Mantoo's first day at school. Until now the four year old had only been called by that name. Her sister turned to her and gave her a choice of three names—Sunaina, Jyoti, Kalpana. 'What do these names mean?' Mantoo asked. After her sister explained the meaning of each name, she chose Kalpana because it meant 'imagination'.

One day, when Kalpana's father returned home from work, he found her waiting at the door. 'Papa, can I ask you something?' she asked as soon as she saw him. 'How do planes fly? How do they stay up in the sky? How do they work?' Little Kalpana had seen a plane fly by that day from the terrace. Her father didn't have the answers to her eager questions, but he promised he would find out.

The next day, he phoned a friend at the Karnal Flying Club, who managed to arrange a tour for them. Her father cycled a delighted Kalpana and her brother to the club. When they got there, his friend took them to a hangar. Kalpana could barely contain her excitement. She ran all around the plane, bombarding him with questions—'Uncle, how does this work? Uncle, what does this do? Uncle, why is this like this?' He laughed and, as a way of answering her questions, flew them in a plane over Karnal. That day, Kalpana discovered her love for flying.

After finishing her pre-engineering course in Karnal, Kalpana went to Punjab University in Chandigarh to study aeronautical engineering. She was the only woman in a class of seventeen. On the first day, one of the professors asked them what they wanted to do with their degree. Most of them said they wanted to work in an aeronautics company. When it was Kalpana's turn, she said, 'I want to be an astronaut.' The professor didn't understand what she meant, so she continued, 'Astronauts go to the moon. I also want to go to the moon!'

Kalpana was the first woman to graduate from Punjab University in aeronautical engineering. She then moved to the US for a masters and a doctorate in aerospace engineering. She began work at the National Aeronautics and Space Administration (NASA) in 1988. At the age of thirty-five, her dream finally came true. She joined a crew of six—again, she was the only woman—on the space shuttle *Columbia* as a robotic arm operator.

Kalpana spoke to the Indian prime minister, I.K. Gujral, from space, describing the starry night sky and the thunderstorms flashing on Earth. It was like a storybook, she said.

A few years later, at age forty-two, Kalpana was part of a seven-member crew on *Columbia* as one of the mission specialists. What none of them knew was that it would be their last flight out.

While taking off from Earth, a piece of foam insulation that protected the rocket from getting too hot broke away from the doomed space shuttle and tore a hole in the left wing.

The crew remained in space for sixteen days. However, as they re-entered the Earth's atmosphere, hot gases entered the damaged wing. The shuttle lost stability and broke apart—in just 73 seconds. All the astronauts on board were killed.

Just before her last mission Kalpana had said, 'It's easy for me to be motivated and inspired by seeing somebody who just goes all out to do something.'

As one who 'went all out' to go to space, Kalpana Chawla's story continues to inspire many more women to dream of flying.

• •

·TEESTA SETALVAD·

In Combat

Three-year-old Teesta walked behind her grandfather, copying his every move. Her dada was India's first Attorney-General; little Teesta wanted to be just like him.

Teesta was born into a family of lawyers. Her great-grandfather, her grandfather and even her father were lawyers. Until she was twelve, Teesta thought that she too would become a lawyer when she grew up.

The house had a large library with books on world history, politics, social science, civil society and science. Teesta's father, Atul, who insisted everyone including his children call him by his name, encouraged her to read as much as she could from their library and not bother with her textbooks.

Teesta listened to the radio and read three newspapers every day. The family discussed politics at the dinner table and Atul encouraged Teesta to air her opinions. Each time, he also presented her with alternate views. When her parents were out for dinner, Teesta would leave long notes about the day's news on the dining table for her father to read when he got back. She didn't want to miss a discussion the following day.

One day, Teesta told Atul she wanted to become a journalist. He encouraged her to start writing for her college newspaper. After college, she got a job at a newspaper. She had a formidable editor who would ruthlessly cut out anything he felt was not newsworthy. But young Teesta stood her ground when she felt her story had merit, and earned his respect.

After some time Teesta moved to another newspaper. Here, she was mentored by a senior journalist. They would go to the Maharashtra State Secretariat and the Municipal Corporation and keenly observe the happenings there. They would also pore over scores of records to

Illustrated by Aparajita Ninan

discover the background and meaning of everything that went on in these institutions. All 'exclusive reports' or front-page stories they worked on were first questioned, debated and rigorously checked.

In the next few years, Teesta wrote extensively about the judicial system, the education system, the Bombay Municipal Corporation and councillors, the courts and the Constitution. She also covered elections and the plight of people in drought-ridden areas.

In 1993, Teesta started a publication called *Communalism Combat* to document communal violence in the country. She found that there was targeted violence against Dalit and Adivasi communities. She cared deeply about this injustice, even as mainstream society remained blind to it. She spoke to many Dalit groups and opened up the *Combat* to powerful Adivasi and Dalit writing. She wanted to make their voices heard and shame the national media into doing the same.

In 2002, there was a wave of communal violence in the form of anti-Muslim riots in Gujarat. Many of the perpetrators were eventually convicted and jailed, partly thanks to the efforts of Teesta's organisation, Citizens for Justice and Peace (CJP). For years, activists and lawyers struggled in the courts to get justice.

Teesta has often said that the justice system in India is aimed at tiring you out so you stop fighting and give up. But if you challenge people in court and continue the fight, as she has for fifteen years, that's when the bullies start to stand down.

Today, CJP is still battling in hostile courts. They offer their legal expertise to a host of human rights defenders—Adivasis, minorities, the LGBTQIA community and anganwadi workers.

Teesta says that conflict can occur even among the best of friends, but all conflicts can be resolved, no matter how serious the differences. How? Through dialogue, debate and discussion.

• •

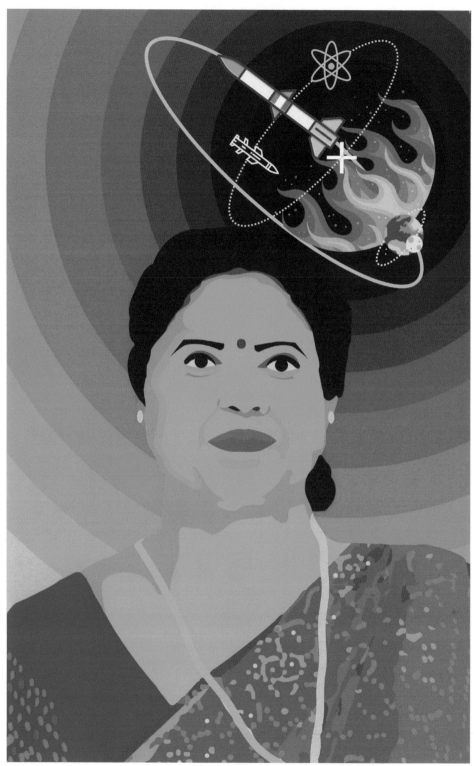

Illustrated by Shivanee Harshey

· TESSY THOMAS ·

Missile Woman

Tessy stared at the sky, fascinated. There was a long, cloud-like trail streaming from the jet that was flying by. What was it? How did it form? Tessy's favourite subjects at school were science and maths—she knew that she wanted to be a scientist someday. Her house was near the Thumba Rocket Launching Station in Thiruvananthapuram, and her dream was to work there when she grew up.

When Tessy was in the eighth grade, her father fell seriously ill. Her mother was a teacher by training but she wasn't working in those days. Tessy recalls her telling them that things could get difficult at any point in life, one just had to be prepared.

Tessy loved school and did extremely well in her studies. With a loan from a bank, she attended the Government Engineering College in Thrissur, where she chose to study electronics. In the final year there was a course on radar systems, and although Tessy didn't know what that was, she went for it, keen to do something different.

One day, she saw an advertisement by the Department of Research and Development Organisation (DRDO) for a guided weapons programme. She applied and was one of ten people to be selected for it. And so she joined the Institute of Armament Technology in Pune to pursue a degree in guided missile technology. This was a turning point in her life.

In 1988, Tessy joined the DRDO in Hyderabad. There were very few women there. She worked with Dr A.P.J. Abdul Kalam, who was the director at the time. The future President of India believed in teamwork and sharing of information and it was from him that she learnt to be a curious and constant learner.

Soon Tessy was assigned to develop navigation and guidance designs for the DRDO's defence programme. In 2011, she became the first woman scientist to head Agni, India's missile programme. She proved—if proof was ever required—that science is not only a man's domain.

But it was never easy. When Agni III was to be launched, her son Tejas was running a temperature of 103° F. He knew his mother was busy, so he didn't tell her. A few days later, Tejas called his father, who was in the Indian Navy and posted in a different city, to tell him he was ill. Tessy still remembers this episode with some regret.

Tessy follows Dr Kalam's mantra: 'All birds find shelter during rain. But the eagle avoids the rain by flying above the clouds.' She believes difficulties will come and go, but we must rise above them.

·DAYAMANI BARLA·

Tribal Activist

Dayamani couldn't concentrate on her schoolwork. How could she, when her family was in such trouble? Some 'upper caste' people from the neighbouring village in Jharkhand had tricked her uneducated parents into signing over their farmland to them. Her parents had sold everything they possessed to go to court and battle it out, but they were losing.

Soon enough, the family fell apart, going their separate ways to work as labourers or domestic help. Only Dayamani and her elder brother stayed back in Arhara. Dayamani was determined to get an education so nobody could ever make a fool of her.

She and her brother worked in neighbouring farms and survived on the little food that they got in return. The jungle around them was rich in resources and they would often forage for leaves, roots, underground tubers and juicy fruits. They sold some of the produce and consumed the rest.

Dayamani stayed in the village till she finished her eighth grade and then joined her mother, who now worked in Ranchi as a maid. It was a tough life. She slept in a cowshed and did all sorts of jobs, including washing utensils at a police station, working at a soap factory and tutoring children, so she could continue her studies. She was sure that education was the only way to fight those who took advantage of uneducated Adivasis like her parents.

Around the time Dayamani finished college, the Bihar government was constructing a dam on the Koel and Karo rivers. Dayamani joined a number of activists and journalists who were protesting the displacement caused by the dams. Eventually the project was stalled. This was her first brush with activism.

Illustrated by Rae Zachariah

Dayamani began to write about the struggles and needs of her community, about women's issues, and the larger problems in society. Along with a few others, she set up a small publication called *Jan Haq*, a newspaper that focused on the problems of the Adivasis.

She also wrote a few articles for *Prabhat Khabar*, another Hindi newspaper. It wasn't easy. If she worked on fifteen stories, only three would get published. Then she won her first award, the Counter Media Award for Rural Journalism, in 2000. She received a cheque and a voice recorder as a prize. Things changed. Now, if she filed fifteen stories, at least thirteen would get published.

But Dayamani wanted to make an even bigger impact. She led protests against steel-manufacturing companies that threatened to displace lakhs of people in the area and take over land that belonged to the Adivasis. She was threatened and put behind bars many times, but she continued her struggle undaunted.

Today, Dayamani and her husband run a little tea-shop called the Jharkhand Hotel, which is their main source of income. She continues to lobby for new policies that will support her community. She believes that children should be encouraged to think not only about themselves, but also about the world they will leave behind—a better place, or worse!

• •

Illustrated by Siddhangana Karmakar

· SHARDA UGRA ·

Writing Sport

Eighteen-month-old Sharda was about to jump off the second-floor balcony when the maid spotted her and screamed. Sharda had just seen the boy downstairs jumping into the garden from his room, and she wanted to do the same. Thankfully, her mother managed to pick her up just in time. The maid was still shocked, but the mother was not surprised. It wasn't the first time little Sharda had displayed an adventurous streak.

Sharda's parents encouraged her to be independent from the very beginning. At thirteen, Sharda would travel on buses and the Bombay local all by herself. The first time she travelled alone, her mother followed her and sat at a little distance from her to make sure she didn't get lost. But Sharda didn't know this.

Every evening, all the children in Sharda's housing colony used to get together to play. Sharda loved sports—badminton, swimming, football, cricket, hockey. But she was terrible at all of them. Often, when she tried to play with the older children, mostly boys, they would get exasperated and send her off the field.

In the early 1980s there was no TV or Internet, but Sharda had a neighbour who bought every sports magazine available in the market. She used to borrow them and read each one cover to cover. Sometimes she would tear out the posters in the magazines and stick them on her walls.

When Sharda was in college, she and her friends occasionally interviewed cricketers who were visiting Bombay. Their first meeting was with the handsome cricketer Imran Khan, and a local paper published the interview. After they had interviewed a few more cricketers, Sharda realised that she was really enjoying this. Right after graduation, she joined a Bombay tabloid as a sports journalist.

At that time, there were no women sports journalists. Once, when Sharda went to Indore to report on a cricket match, she found that there was a tent for the press and two little sheds that were meant to be dressing rooms for the teams. She was the only woman in the press box. After a while, she went to the organisers and asked them where the washroom was. They were flummoxed. They had made arrangements for the press-box seats, the chai and samosas, but the loo? After much deliberation, they requested her to use the bathroom in one of the dressing rooms.

Today, Sharda is one of the most respected sports journalists in India. She has worked for several major publications, both Indian and international. She has written over 3000 articles and co-authored two books on cricket. She has won the Sports Journalists' Federation of India award for sports writing and other prestigious journalism awards. A passionate cricket fan, she has seen cricket played in nine countries and reported on two Olympics.

But life isn't always easy for Sharda. She has an illness called multiple sclerosis, an auto-immune disease that attacks the central nervous system. There are times when she has to stop everything and go into hospital, or just stay still and be patient.

She says, 'MS is an uncomfortable travelling companion, but so far it has been a considerate one. It makes me wait, but lets me get to where I wanted to be in the first place.'

Sharda believes that one needs to be interested in the sport, not just in the players, if one wants to be a sports journalist. Sport lasts forever, stars can fade or disappoint.

● ●

· BARKHA DUTT ·

Face of Prime Time

Barkha was watching her mother argue with her school principal. She had wanted to take woodcraft as a subject, but the faculty had denied her. 'What do you mean woodcraft is not suitable for a girl?' her mother said sharply. Barkha's mother, Prabha, was India's first woman reporter to cover war and conflict. She was used to standing up to people who said no to her, and Barkha learnt the lesson early.

School for Barkha was about reading, theatre, elocution and writing for the school magazine. Her mother passed away when she was thirteen and her father had to bring up two rebellious teenage girls on his own. While they were given a lot of freedom, they kept pushing for more. Barkha was particularly inspired by the character of Jo March in the classic *Little Women*. She even went to a nearby salon and had her long hair cut in an act of rebellion, just like Jo does in the book.

Barkha thought she would become a lawyer or a documentary filmmaker but fate pushed her towards her mother's career—journalism. Her first job was with NDTV which, at the time, produced a thirty-minute English news bulletin on Doordarshan. She joined as a technical producer and, since it was a small outfit, was soon asked to start reporting as well.

Her first assignment was in a village in Rajasthan, reporting the case of a woman—Bhanwari Devi—who'd been violently attacked by a mob of men for trying to stop a child marriage. The experience changed Barkha. Her naïve urban notions of feminism and caste were severely challenged and she came away with a deeper understanding of rural India.

When the Kargil War broke out in 1999, Barkha wanted to be where the action was and not in the TV studio. She convinced her employers to let her go to Kargil and also took special permission from the Indian Army. The army told her that they couldn't give her any 'women's toilet facilities' or special protection, but she was undeterred.

Illustrated by Ayesha Broacha

The war was tough and brutal. She saw death all around her, but Barkha trained herself to control her emotions so that no one would think she was not strong enough for the assignment. Her reportage on Kargil won her many accolades, including from the then army chief.

Barkha believes that every good journalist should have a special area of interest and she made Jammu and Kashmir hers. She spent almost half of every month there for over a decade and reported on the problems in the region—on war, insurgency and terrorism. She also covered stories of conflict in Libya, Afghanistan and Pakistan.

In 2010, Barkha and several other journalists came under attack for their association with a powerful corporate spokesperson. Barkha was angry because she felt she was subjected to unusually intense scrutiny, in a way that her male colleagues were not.

Barkha moved away from TV journalism after twenty-one years and now has her own digital media company.

Her advice to young people? 'Challenge yourself constantly. When you climb a mountain and reach the peak, find another peak. Don't let fame or loyalty get in the way.'

·VANDANA GOPIKUMAR & · VAISHNAVI JAYAKUMAR

Giving Hope

Vandana was crying. She and her family were visiting the Guruvayur temple in Kerala for the early morning darshan. She was ravenous, but her parents had told her that she could eat only after the darshan. When they approached the tiny inner sanctum of the temple, a priest quietly handed Vandana a banana. She immediately stopped crying.

Her parents had taught Vandana to believe in the power of magic, that if she wanted something badly enough, she would get it. They taught her that she could will things to happen.

Vandana's father was in the Air Force and they moved homes often. This meant that each time, she had to leave behind her friends and the roadside dogs that she considered family.

Her parents never told her in so many words to share things or to treat everyone as an equal. They demonstrated these concepts to her through their own behaviour. Her mother had a strong sense of justice and fairness. She made friends with beggar women and their children and they would all go and eat ice cream together. The children of their house staff had all the privileges Vandana had. She grew up believing that everyone was part of one big community.

Meanwhile, fifteen-year-old Vaishnavi had just moved from Calcutta to Chennai. She wasn't happy—she had moved from a really friendly city to an entirely new place where she knew no one. Often, feeling lonely, she would climb up to the terrace and sit there for hours. Then she would come back and smile and pretend to be happy. She could never tell her parents how she felt. But as she got busy at school, she began to feel better.

Vandana met Vaishnavi in college, and it was the start of a remarkable relationship.

One day, at the Institute of Mental Health, where Vandana was training, she met a young woman who said to her, 'Look at the bag you are carrying, and your fancy clothes. Look at the power and privilege you have. Because of my mental health issues, my husband has abandoned me. I don't have the freedom or opportunity to be you. But remember, at any time you can become me!' This outburst had a huge impact on Vandana. She told Vaishnavi about it, and they went to meet the woman together.

Another time, Vandana and Vaishnavi saw a woman outside their college. She was running up and down the road, half naked and with matted hair. They could tell from her behaviour that she was mentally ill. They also noticed that most people around them were uncomfortable. Some were scared, some looked worried—and some just didn't care.

This incident affected both of them deeply. They began noticing more people with mental health issues on the streets. They realised that destitute women with mental illness were the most marginalised in society. When they visited a mental institute, they found that the male patients had visitors—the women had none.

As qualified professionals—Vandana had a degree in mental health care and Vaishnavi in management—they decided this would be their career goal: working with people with mental health issues. In 1993, they set up a centre in Chennai called The Banyan.

They started with thirteen patients in a small rented house. As the number of patients started to grow, the then chief minister of Tamil Nadu, J. Jayalalithaa, read about their work in a newspaper and called them for a meeting. She allocated some land for The Banyan and, whenever she met the two young women, would ask about their patients.

One of the women in the institution, Ramkumari, was from the little village of Pratapgarh in Rajasthan. She kept asking Vandana and Vaishnavi

Illustrated by Osheen Siva

to let her go home to her husband and children. She had even stitched clothes for her children. The girls agreed and took her to the village, but once there, Ramkumari couldn't recognise anything. They took her to the local police station to see if there was a missing persons report. Just when they were about to give up, a man on a bicycle recognized Ramkumari; he asked them to follow him to her home. In the distance they could see a house decorated with lights. When they reached the house, the first thing they saw was a picture of Ramkumari with a garland around it. Her family thought she was dead.

As Ramkumari stood there uncertainly, her children rushed to hug her, weeping. Ramkumari took some time to understand that her children had grown up—she had been missing for six years. Her family was ecstatic to have her back—especially because it was the day of her oldest daughter's wedding!

It was a magical moment for Vandana and Vaishnavi. They now knew that their patients could be rehabilitated and could finally go home to live in their communities. They shared Ramkumari's remarkable story with the media and it helped change at least a few people's perceptions about mental health patients.

Today, patients at The Banyan live with a sense of hope. For those without a home to go back to, Vaishnavi and Vandana have introduced a community living project. Four or five women are placed with a personal assistant who helps them adjust to life in a neighbourhood. Eventually the women start becoming self-sufficient.

Both Vandana and Vaishnavi have had mental health challenges of their own. This has increased their awareness of the need to reach out to others for support.

There is no clear dividing line between sanity and insanity, says Vaishnavi. She wishes people would stop using the words 'psycho' and 'loser' as insults. Some of the best ideas of our time have come from people who have had mental health challenges—Virginia Woolf, Abraham Lincoln, Picasso.

Vandana says that children should be taught to treat others—no matter who they are—the way they would like to be treated themselves: with dignity. She loves the African greeting Sawubona, which means 'I see you'. She wishes more people would stop to see and connect with those around them.

• •

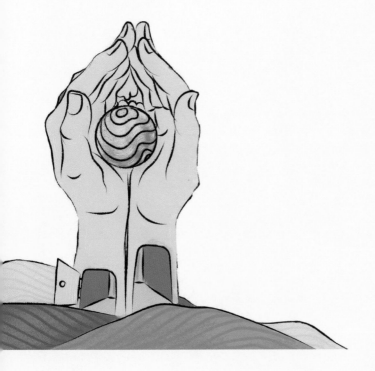

Illustrated by Shikha Nambiar

·IROM SHARMILA CHANU·

Iron Lady

Sharmila was walking to school in her red-and-white uniform with her siblings. The school was a couple of kilometres away and Sharmila wondered why she had to go there every day. She would much rather stay home and play hide-and-seek. Tired, she sat at the foot of a banyan tree and refused to walk any further. Her siblings scolded her, but she ignored them. Realising that threats had no effect on her, they resorted to begging and cajoling. Sharmila refused to budge. Exasperated, they left her under the tree. Eight hours later, after a long day at school, they found her still sitting under the tree. Such was her willpower.

Sharmila wasn't very good at studies—in fact, she stopped attending school after the eleventh grade. She was a quiet girl and led a simple life cycling around the village, writing poetry and visiting friends.

In 2000, while interning for a month with Human Rights Alert, Sharmila visited a neighbouring village, along with advocates from the commission, to meet twenty-five-year-old Mercy Kabui.

A few months earlier, some men from the Central Reserve Police Force (CRPF) had entered Mercy's home, dragged her to the back of the house and raped her. Sharmila was horrified by the story but quietly did her job, which was to translate for the advocates.

A few months later, army vehicles were passing through the village of Malom when there was an explosion. A group of rebels had been waiting for the convoy. One vehicle was damaged and two men were injured. The army responded by entering the village and firing randomly at civilians, including students. Imphal was shut down and a curfew was imposed.

Sharmila heard accounts of atrocities by the forces and the cruelty people had suffered at the hands of some soldiers. A law called the Armed

Forces Special Powers Act (AFSPA) enabled the Indian Armed Forces to arrest or kill people whom they suspected of threatening them—or peace in the area—without fear of prosecution. They didn't need proof; mere suspicion was enough.

In November 2000, a day after the attack in Malom, twenty-eight-year-old Sharmila went into the bamboo grove in her compound and ate two boxes of sweets. No one knew that it was the last morsel of food she would eat for years. She then went to her mother, Sakhi Devi, and asked for her blessings. 'I am going to do something for my land,' she said. She then vowed not to eat or drink or comb her hair until AFSPA was revoked.

After three days, the police arrested Sharmila on a charge of attempted suicide and put her in judicial custody. They then took her to a hospital where they fed her by forcing a tube up her nose. She met her mother only once after this, because she was afraid that her resolve would weaken if she saw her sad face again.

Thus began Sharmila's new life. For the next sixteen years she refused to eat. She would be released from jail, re-arrested and force-fed over and over again. During her time in custody and in hospital, she read voraciously, and wrote letter after letter to heads of government and human rights groups to seek the repeal of AFSPA, but to no avail. She won many awards during this time. Her protest is still the longest hunger strike known to the world.

In 2016, Sharmila broke her fast with honey and water followed by rice soup. She announced that she would continue her fight through political means and contested the next general election from Imphal, only to suffer a terrible defeat.

AFSPA has still not been repealed. Sharmila says she intends to continue the fight against it, although she no longer lives in Manipur.

● ●

·RITU DALMIA·

Food Diva

Twelve-year-old Ritu was listening to her teacher talk about apartheid in South Africa. 'There were the fair people,' the teacher said, pointing to herself. 'And there were the dark people,' she continued, pointing at the class. 'The English-speaking ones—and the natives. There was discrimination against the dark, native people.'

The irony of the statement hit Ritu and her classmates and Ritu started giggling. Unfortunately, giggling always made her snort. As she started to snort loudly, the rest of the students joined her. The teacher was furious at the disruption. As a punishment, Ritu was made to climb into a large dustbin till the period was over. It was a spot she found herself in many times over the next few years!

Ritu's parents travelled a great deal on work. While her three siblings would ask them to bring back all sorts of toys, Ritu asked for blocks of cheese. As a child, she enjoyed reading cookbooks and looking at pictures of food. Every time she tried her hand at cooking, her older brother would give her a bit of his pocket money. Ritu discovered quite early that she loved food and cooking and, best of all, that she could actually make money from it!

Ritu also knew early that she wanted to be her own boss. Whenever she went to visit her grandfather, she would swivel in his big chair and pretend to be 'boss-boss'. She attended college for exactly one day before deciding that it was not for her. She joined her father's business and, at sixteen, insisted on being sent on business trips all over the world. She went—alone—to buy machinery, sell marble and explore the local cuisines on the side. She loved travelling and especially loved Italy and Italian food. Fresh basil, olive oil, pasta—she delighted in their flavours.

Ritu quit the business when she was twenty-one, following a disagreement with her father, and confided in her mother about wanting to open an

Illustrated by Shivanee Harshey

Italian restaurant in Delhi. They knew her father would be appalled. A Marwari girl from a traditional family starting a restaurant, one that served non-vegetarian food? It was unheard of.

Ritu's first restaurant, Mezzaluna, opened in Delhi when most people didn't know what Italian food was. The few who did come to her restaurant wanted to know why the smoked salmon was cold. They asked for spicy pickled onions with their main course. Ritu was furious and refused to serve them. She decided to leave India and open a restaurant in London instead.

The restaurant, Vama, was a great success, but Ritu was in love with a woman in India. So she moved back to Delhi and set up the now popular Diva.

Ritu realised that while her dreams were big, there were very few people in India who were qualified to work in her restaurant. She has since trained over 500 young underprivileged people and has opened more restaurants in Delhi and Milan.

Ritu caters for high-profile events in the country and abroad, and is the author of three bestselling Italian cookbooks for the Indian market. She is without doubt the first Indian chef-entrepreneur to be so success-ful. Today, most of her senior management and head chefs are women.

Ritu credits her success to her ability to learn from failure. Each time she makes a mistake, she picks herself up and becomes better at what she does.

• •

Illustrated by Sanchita Jain

·SONI SORI·

Conscience Keeper

Five-year-old Soni was watching the clock while her cows grazed. At about four o'clock, she shepherded the cows to the local school in her village in Dantewada. She ran up to the cook who had just finished serving porridge to the school children and said, 'Can I clean your pots?' The man handed over the pots to her. Soni sat in a corner and scraped off and ate every little bit of the porridge left in the pots before cleaning them.

One day, the teacher at the school noticed the little girl who grazed her cows near the school every day at the same time. When he asked her why, she reluctantly said, 'For the porridge.' He laughed and said, 'If you want to eat porridge, come to school and study.' She said, 'No. If I come to school, who will take care of the cows?'

The teacher, however, was persistent and spoke to her father. That's how Soni started going to school. After a year she was sent to a boarding school where she studied till the twelfth grade. She then began work as a teacher near her village and, in 2006, she became a hostel warden for an ashram school.

During this time the Naxals had slowly started infiltrating the region. The authorities would arrest innocent people from Soni's village for questioning, accusing them of being Naxals. The villagers turned to Soni for help since she was a teacher. She soon found herself speaking to the police on behalf of her Adivasi community.

By 2008, there was a huge Naxal presence in the area, which led to increased policing. In the summer holidays, the school buildings would be taken over and occupied by police forces.

One day, a man approached Soni and the other teachers and said that the Naxal leader wanted to meet them. Soni was scared but the villagers said to her, 'He is just a person like you, go and meet him.' She was the only teacher who went.

She found herself in the middle of a 'jan adalat' of thousands of people. The leader said to her, 'Madam, the police are staying in your ashram school. We are going to come and break down all of your school buildings.' Soni was horrified. What would the children do?

Gathering up her courage, she said, 'Dada, what are you fighting for?' He said, 'We are fighting for our people, for our resources, our land, our rights.' She said, 'But the children are also ours. How can you say you are fighting for us by destroying what they need?'

He didn't answer for a while. Finally, he told Soni he would spare two of the hostels. Before she left he warned her, 'If we get to hear you are sheltering police there, we will bring you back and kill you too.'

Soni thought hard. This compromise would mean that she would save the residence of at least 150 children, so she agreed. The Naxals destroyed the other hostels and left hers alone.

Soni ran the school for a couple of years, but the authorities were suspicious. How was her school thriving? They accused Soni of sheltering Naxals and supplying them with weapons. They arrested her family members on false charges and accused her of being a go-between for the Naxals and a large corporate house. They began to harass her for information and finally trapped her in eight false cases.

She came to Delhi then, but was arrested. When she was presented before the judge, she pleaded, 'Sir, arrest me, but please put me in Tihar jail. Do not send me to Chhattisgarh. I will be harassed.'

The police promised the judge they would treat Soni 'like a sister' and the judge convinced her to go back. Back in Dantewada, she was sent for two days of remand during which she was mercilessly tortured and raped. She was due to be presented before a judge, but since the evidence of torture was visible on her body, she was persuaded to sign some papers and taken back to jail without seeing the judge. Twenty-five days later, when she came before the judge, she wept and said, 'Madam, you didn't even check to see if I was okay after my remand? You didn't see what they did to me. What justice will you give me?'

There were rumours that Soni was lying. However, from video footage and confessions by policemen off camera, it seemed clear that she had been tortured. She was in jail for the next two years.

After her release Soni went home to find that the Naxals had captured her father's land and attacked him for being a police informer. She found the Naxal leader and said to him, 'Dada, you say you fight for the people. What is the difference between you and the authorities who take our lands and harm us? We have farmed all our life. What will we do without our land?' The Naxals eventually returned her father's land and the police became suspicious again.

Despite the efforts of human rights activists who have been supporting Soni's cause, she still has a police case pending against her. She says, 'No one has bothered to understand that you can win hearts and battles even through dialogue.'

Soni says that as a child, she could walk home safely at night. Today, no woman can step out for fear of being molested. And so she continues her battle for the safety and rights of the people of Bastar.

• •

Illustrated by Shikha Nambiar

·ANSHU JAMSENPA·

Climbing Everest

Seven-year-old Anshu was dancing in front of some guests who were visiting her home. A natural entertainer, she loved dancing and mimicking people. That day, her dance was a bit odd. The guests asked, 'What kind of dance is this?' Although Anshu had made it up herself, she replied, 'It's from my mother's family.' The guests laughed but Anshu's mother was quite upset. She later scolded Anshu for embarrassing her and her artistic Monpa tribe by making up that story!

Anshu loved all sorts of challenges. Once, in the play area of her school, instead of sitting on the swing, she climbed up the frame and started to walk across it. She fell and hurt herself, of course. But she remained an adventurer—the accident did nothing to curb her spirit.

She got married while she was still in school and soon had two children. Her husband, Tsering, ran a Himalayan adventure company in Bomdila. One day, Anshu decided she wanted to go mountaineering too, and made a first attempt on a steep rock face. The instructors at the company encouraged her and said she showed great promise. That was all the push she needed. Over the next couple of months, she took three mountaineering courses and also began to help her husband with the mountaineering business. Soon she started going on short expeditions. In a few years, she had climbed over thirteen peaks in India and abroad.

Mountaineering changed Anshu's way of thinking. People from her small border town in Arunachal Pradesh couldn't understand why she was obsessed with climbing mountains. She couldn't explain it either. But she knew that mountaineering builds character and brings positivity to one's life, and she decided she would prove this to those around her, especially the children.

In 2011, Anshu went on an Everest expedition and successfully climbed from base camp to summit, twice in ten days. She could have done it in less, but the local team in Nepal didn't support her. They wanted someone from their own country to go first. Anshu tried to double ascend again in the year 2014, but an avalanche struck and sixteen mountaineers lost their lives. Undeterred, she decided to give it another shot in 2015. As fate would have it, there was a devastating earthquake that killed twenty-two mountaineers. She escaped unhurt but her Everest mission had to be called off.

Anshu didn't give up, though. In April 2017, she scaled Everest twice in five days and created a world record, becoming the only woman to have climbed Everest twice in five days. Finally, people started recognising her achievements.

Anshu is still climbing mountains and seeking her next adventure. She encourages children to respect nature and train to climb mountains. She says mountaineering helps people deal with their personal challenges and builds mental and physical strength. She remains the only Indian woman to have climbed Mount Everest five times.

••

·GAURI SAWANT·

Transgender Mom

Ganesh was born on Ganesh Chaturthi to a police officer and a teacher. As a child, he used to play with the girls in his locality. He would run after them and pull the bright red ribbons from their hair. The neighbours would laugh at him and say, 'Look at the father—so masculine—and look at the son—a joker!'

When the boy was nine, his mother died. His father knew that Ganesh was not like other boys but he didn't know how to handle him. One day, the two of them went shopping for his school uniform. At the store, there was a large mannequin wearing a sari. Ganesh was curious to see what was underneath the sari, so he lifted it up. Much to his father's embarrassment, the shopkeeper asked Ganesh what he was doing. From that day on, his father stopped speaking to him.

At some point, he was sent away to his grandmother's house. Ganesh would often wear his nani's blouse, bunch up his hair in a towel so it looked like a jooda, and drape a sari to complete the look. He loved watching the pop singer Usha Uthup on TV and wanted to be just like her, with her deep voice, big bindi and beautiful saris.

When his grandmother died, Ganesh moved to Bombay to be with his father. But their war of silence continued.

Ganesh often met people from the hijra community on his way to college. As a way of making friends, he gave them his grandmother's saris. They said to him, 'Don't come to us. Study hard.'

One day, when he was nineteen, Ganesh woke up to an open door and thought his father wanted him out of the house. He walked all the way to the hijra colony, which was many kilometres away. His friends took him in and fed him, but he was shocked at the way they lived. He was used

147

Illustrated by Anjul Dandekar

to fragrant basmati rice and stainless steel plates; here, he had to eat fat broken rice from an aluminium plate and drink water from a matka. Unable to adjust to this lifestyle, he went back home after two weeks. That's when his sister told him that his father had bought him a small flat in another suburb and would pay for his groceries and a maid. Ganesh would now live alone.

A little later, Ganesh began working at Humsafar, an organisation dedicated to the welfare of the LGBTQ community—the first of its kind. By now he knew he wasn't gay. He felt like a woman in a man's body and was fascinated by cross-dressers and drag queens. In his early twenties, he had his testes removed and started taking female hormones. He shaped his eyebrows and had his body hair removed. And he began to dress like a woman.

That year, Ganesh's sister refused to tie a rakhi on his hand. She told him that she never wanted to meet him again and that he would be a bad influence on her children. Grief-stricken, Ganesh cried all night.

After three years of counselling, Ganesh had a Sex Reassignment Surgery (SRS) and Gauri was born.

Gauri started an NGO with a few others and called it Sakhi Char Chowghi. They promoted safe sex and provided counselling to people from the transgender and hijra communities.

One day, in the area where Gauri worked, an HIV positive sex worker died and there was talk of selling her five-year-old daughter in Kolkata. Gauri decided to adopt the child as her own and named her Gayatri Gauri Sawant.

Gauri is now raising funds to build Aajicha Ghar, a home for the abandoned children of sex workers. She has become well known for her work and has even appeared on *Kaun Banega Crorepati* where she met her childhood idol, Usha Uthup. She says she was more excited to see Usha than Amitabh Bachchan!

Gauri regrets the fact that while people from the transgender and hijra communities are recognised by the government as the third gender and are entitled to the same rights as every other citizen, they are discriminated against in daily life.

Gauri is happiest when her daughter comes back from boarding school. Motherhood, she says, is the best feeling in the world.

• •

· MITHALI RAJ ·

Batting for India

Eight-year-old Mithali loved sleeping late into the morning, but her father insisted on every single person in the household waking up early. Not just that, she had to accompany him and her brother to his cricket coaching every day. Poor Mithali would blearily carry her schoolbooks along so she could do her homework as she watched.

One summer vacation, her father enrolled Mithali in the camp that her brother attended. As she was the only girl there, the coaches and trainers used to let her go first in the batting order. When they saw how good she was, they told her father to enrol her in a professional camp.

Luckily, the new camp was in her school in Hyderabad, which was well known for having produced some of the best cricket players in the state. Mithali would leave home at 4.30 a.m. for practice and get to class by 8.30 a.m. After the exertions of the morning, she would often fall asleep in the middle of a lesson. The teachers, however, were understanding—they would send her to the back of the room to doze for a bit!

Because she had such a hectic schedule, Mithali missed several exams. When she was twelve, she had to sit her final exams during the summer vacation. Since her classmates had taken the same exams already, they discussed the papers at length, so Mithali knew what the questions would be. But to everyone's surprise, she barely passed! When her mother asked her why she hadn't got better marks despite knowing all the questions, Mithali told her that it wouldn't have been fair to her classmates, who had studied all year and didn't know the questions in advance.

Soon Mithali started to play for the state of Andhra Pradesh. When she was only sixteen, she was selected for the national women's team. In her first One Day International (ODI) match in 1999, she scored 114 runs not out. But it was a tough life for the first few years and she felt very lonely, being the youngest in the team. She was playing with stalwarts like

Illustrated by Joanna Mendes

Purnima Rau and Anjum Chopra. When the team travelled and lost matches, it was hard for her to deal with the disappointment.

Mithali would go home between tournaments for a few days, but her mother barely saw her growing up. Her parents were confident, however, that she would grow up to be a good person.

Mithali was soon breaking records everywhere. In 2004, she was made captain of the Indian team. She spent time understanding her players, crafting strategy and attending meetings. She believes that effective communication is essential to forming a great team.

For years, not many people watched the matches played by the Indian women's cricket team. That changed in 2017 with the ICC Women's World Cup. Influenced by the clever use of social media and smart marketing, more people watched women's cricket than ever before.

In an early match against Australia, Mithali broke the world record for most runs in ODIs, scoring more than 6000 runs, but they lost the game. The team wanted to celebrate her achievement, but Mithali stayed focused on preparations for their next match against New Zealand. When they returned to India with the runners-up trophy, Mithali was introduced everywhere as the woman who had the highest runs in ODIs. Only then did she realise the magnitude of her achievement.

Today, Mithali is the most capped woman ODI player in the world. From rookie player to a mature, level-headed captain, one thing has not changed for Mithali over the years: the joy of walking into a match to play for the country. That, she says, motivates her every day to do her best.

• •

Illustrated by Tara Anand

154

·MANGTE CHUNGNEIJANG·
MARY KOM

Boxing Champ

Chungneijang grew up in a poor household in Kangathei in Manipur, the eldest of three siblings. Her father, a landless farmer, made just enough to feed his family. She helped her father plough the fields with a bullock. It was a difficult task, but young Chungneijang managed quite easily, and this never ceased to amaze the villagers. In the evenings, the family would go to her uncle's house and watch films on a video cassette recorder. Chungneijang loved watching martial art movies; Bruce Lee, Jet Li and Jackie Chan were her favourites.

Chungneijang's father was determined to send his children to an English-medium school. Though she was an average student, Chungneijang excelled in sports and participated in every sporting event in the school. Seeing her focus on sport, her father was worried. He wanted his daughter to have the opportunities he'd never had to study. He moved the children to a new school. Chungneijang was thrilled because it had an even bigger playground! She continued to do so well that the school principal asked her father to take her to the Sports Authority of India (SAI) in Imphal.

Chungneijang's father first took her to meet a local athletics coach. After trying athletics, which she did not enjoy, the sixteen year old left for the SAI in Imphal. She tried her hand at various sports there, but none excited her. Since she loved the martial arts, she found her way into the newly formed boxing academy in Imphal and trained with the coaches there for the next few years.

As people found her name hard to pronounce, a friend advised Chungneijang that she should adopt a 'second' name. She chose Mary because it was Christian, and also easy to pronounce and remember. Her parents didn't know about the name change, or about the fact that she had taken up boxing.

Mary won the gold medal at the Women's Boxing Championship in Manipur in 2000. Her father overheard a few men in the village talking about the 'Kom girl' and was puzzled—the only Kom girl at the academy he knew was his daughter! He immediately called her home and questioned her. When the truth came out, Mary's parents' first reaction was to worry—what if she was injured during a match? And wouldn't it hamper her marriage prospects? But Mary was adamant and when they saw that she was determined, they decided to support her.

Mary participated in tournaments all over India. In 2001, she was selected for an international competition in the US—the AIBA World Boxing Championship—where she won a silver medal. It was very cold and, through her stay in Pennsylvania, Mary was tired. She didn't like the food and could barely eat anything. She lost two kilos, which she felt lost her the gold medal. Sometimes she thought she was being punished because she had fought with her father before leaving for the US.

When she returned, people back home celebrated her victory. She received money from the Government of Manipur and used it to buy some land for her father. In that same year, Mary got married—to a footballer friend she had met in Delhi. Onler Karong was also from Manipur. Mary continued to win medals and received the Arjuna Award in 2003 and the Padma Shri in 2005.

Two years later, she had twins. Leaving her children in the care of her husband and his family, Mary soon returned to her boxing camps. Although she missed the children terribly and her body was constantly aching, she persisted. She worked on her fitness and diet and went on to win her fifth consecutive gold medal at the AIBA World Championship.

Mary's dream was to win an Olympic medal. In 2012, she went to London and won a bronze medal in the 48-kilo category. This was India's first Olympic medal in women's boxing. She came back to an ecstatic country!

In 2018, she defied the odds by winning a gold at the Commomwealth Games, at the age of thirty-five.

The MC Mary Kom Regional Boxing Academy for underprivileged children in Imphal seeks to train a new generation of boxing champs. Mary's students have started winning medals and many have been sponsored by the Olympic Gold Quest. She dreams of making it a world-class academy someday.

• •

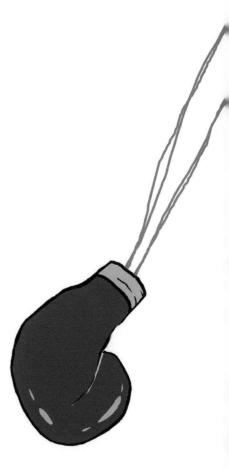

Illustrated by Anjul Dandekar

· SANIA MIRZA ·

Tennis Ace

Sania was watching her father play a game of tennis in Ohio, USA. She and her twin cousins were acting as ball-persons. After he finished, Sania and her cousins decided to hit a few balls. Since Sania was small, the ball barely went over the net. Her cousins teased and bullied her off the court, but Sania was already in love with the sport. She asked her mother to send her for tennis classes. But they were expensive and her parents couldn't afford them at the time. When they moved back to India, the first thing her mother did was enrol Sania in tennis, swimming and roller-skating classes. She was thrilled!

The coach at Nizam Club had never seen a six year old hit a ball with so much power. He called Sania's father, Imran, to come and watch. When Imran saw her potential, he started to take her game seriously. The coach told him that Sania could become a state champion. Imran started coaching her then, to develop her mental agility and strength.

Sania began playing in club tournaments, then state tournaments, and then on the All India Tennis Association circuit. Her parents used to get into their car and drive to the match location with Sania and her little sister, staying overnight in inexpensive lodges. All the hard work paid off when Sania won a spot in the Under-14 team to play for India.

The baby of the team, Sania dominated the circuit, winning six out of eight matches that year. At the age of twelve, she became No. 1 in the Under-14 category and was soon No. 1 in the Under-18 category too. Titles continued to come her way. In 2001, at the age of fourteen, she became the youngest player to compete at any event at Wimbledon.

In 2003, sixteen-year-old Sania spotted the young Russian Alisa Kleybanova and asked her to be her doubles partner. They played together beautifully and, despite their nervousness, went all the way to the finals of the Wimbledon Doubles Junior Championship. It was the first time an Indian girl had won the Junior Wimbledon.

Over the next decade, Sania's career as a singles player took her to No. 27 in the world rankings. In 2012, she decided to retire from singles after multiple injuries to her knees and wrist. She started playing mixed doubles with ace Indian player Mahesh Bhupati and won her first Grand Slam title with him: the Australian Open.

She then partnered with former World No. 1 Martina Hingis and the pair took the tennis world by storm. In 2015, Sania became the No. 1 player in women's doubles. That same year, she became the first Indian woman to ever win a Wimbledon final, when Martina and she won the women's doubles.

Sania's life off the court was eventful too. Her identity as a young Muslim girl playing a sport that required her to dress in short skirts came up for scrutiny every once in a while. In 2010, when she married Pakistan cricketer Shoaib Malik, she was stalked by the media in both countries. But Sania and her family stood firm, refusing to be cowed by this public bullying.

In 2013, she set up the Sania Mirza Tennis Academy in Hyderabad. She spends a lot of time supporting and grooming youngsters from rural India to play tennis. In 2017, she also started the Sania Mirza Grassroot Level Academy for children between three and eight.

'Dreams are the seeds that lead to all achievement,' says Sania. 'But all dreams must be backed by hard work and perseverance.'

• •

·KARAMJYOTI DALAL·

Para-athlete

The school bus was late, so eight-year-old Jyotu and her classmate decided to start walking home. When the bus reached Jyotu's house in Mount Abu without her in it, her mother and brother were worried. Where could she be? When Jyotu finally ambled in, her anxious mother slapped her. 'Don't you ever walk back alone,' she said, 'the world's a dangerous place for girls.'

Jyotu was so upset, she ran out of the house and up the hill. Her mother and friends followed, and tried to call her back. But she refused to return. She wanted her mother to put her hands to her ears and say sorry. Her helpless mother had to agree before they could all find their way home.

Jyotu's father served in the Indian Army. When he was transferred to Kashmir, he sent the family back home to Rohtak. Karamjyoti played many sports in school. Kabaddi was her favourite, and she was very good at it. Her family, though, wasn't happy. They didn't think it was proper for a girl to play outdoors. But she continued to play kabaddi even in college.

Karamjyoti had epilepsy, a condition that sometimes caused her body to shake violently. One day, she was sitting with her family on the first-floor terrace of their house, when an epilepsy attack struck. Before her father could reach her, Karamjyoti fell off the terrace. She was twenty-one.

The family rushed her to hospital. When the doctors operated on her, they found that her spinal cord had been crushed. She would never walk again, they said. Her parents, however, refused to lose hope. Her brother persuaded her to study further so she could keep herself meaning-fully occupied, and she ended up earning a diploma in education.

One day, a relative suggested to Karamjyoti that she could try para-athletics as she'd been so good at sports. She took her to a stadium where para-athletes were training in shot put, discus and javelin. Karamjyoti was fascinated. She managed to impress the coaches at the tryouts and,

Illustrated by Tanya Eden

with her father's support, enrolled at the academy. She started training every day and qualified for the Asian Games in shot put, javelin and discus. At the championships in 2014, she won two bronze medals.

Karamjyoti then applied for the Target Olympic Podium Scheme (TOPS), a government programme aimed at giving athletes financial assistance and better access to coaching. No para-athlete had applied for it before, but her proposal was accepted, and she was sent to train in Finland for two years.

Karamjyoti qualified for the Rio Olympics in 2016, but all of her throws were disqualified—the officials said her legs had moved a little while she threw the discus. She had not known about this rule and was deeply upset. In 2017, when she competed in the World Para Athletics Championships, she tied six belts tightly round her legs so they couldn't move. As a paraplegic, she had no control over her motor activity. She observed all the other participants closely and noticed one whose legs had moved. She informed the committee and they declared a foul. Karamjyoti won the bronze medal.

There was a time when girls were not given the same importance as boys in Karamjyoti's large joint family. She had relatives who insisted that it was not right for girls to compete in sports. However, when she started to win matches, they began to treat her with respect. Karamjyoti says this was something she had always wanted, even as a child.

Karamjyoti regrets the fact that all persons with disabilities are viewed through the same lens. Not everyone in a wheelchair has the same condition, she points out. One may be able to move her legs, while another may be completely paralysed. She wishes people would be more sensitive to those with disabilities.

•• •

SAINA NEHWAL & P.V. SINDHU

Conquering Stars

The mood was upbeat at the Gopichand Badminton Academy in Hyderabad. The younger players were excited. They had been watching Saina Nehwal and P.V. Sindhu beat their formidable Chinese opponents consistently. Both women had been playing badminton for several years now, and everyone there knew the important landmarks along their journey to success.

When she was little, Saina would spend the odd evening at the Faculty Club in Hissar, eating chips and an omelette, watching her parents play badminton. Her mother had been a state player for Haryana. Saina came for the food and her friends. Badminton didn't really interest her. She preferred running around, climbing trees and playing cricket.

Saina's father, an agricultural scientist, moved to Hyderabad with the family when she was eight. It was 1988 and Saina was bored in the new city—she had no friends, and she missed being physically active. She tried karate in a neighbourhood class for a year and even got a brown belt, but found it hard going.

One day, her father took her to the stadium where he played badminton, and asked if the coaches would enrol Saina in the summer camp. Coaches Nani Prasad and Goverdhan Reddy said they were too late. Camp selections had been done. Her father insisted they at least watch Saina play. Luckily Saina's first shot was a smash. She was in.

Even though she was very young, the coaches were hard on her. Running up and down stairs, cross-country racing, skipping—she had to do it all. She would train at the camp in the morning and with her mother at home in the evening. Saina was happy. Her days were full and she was never bored. She continued to train after she was done with the camp. This meant waking up at 4 a.m., taking a bus to the stadium, training for two hours, going to school, and leaving again for the stadium. It would be 9 p.m. by the time she got home. Everyone would be tired, including her parents. Saina would cry and her mother would massage her aching legs, but the next day she would be back and training. She had begun to love the game.

In 1999, Saina started playing—and winning—in the Under-10 category at the district level. Her mother would tell her, 'Saina, you have to get an Olympic medal for me.'

When she was eleven, Coach Mohammed Arif made Saina focus on stamina, fitness and outdoor training. She says this laid the foundation for her ability to play long matches later.

When Saina was thirteen, she started training under Pullela Gopichand, a retired player who was planning to open his own academy. She trained with the Zen-like Gopi for years. He taught her visualisation and meditation to help her focus.

At sixteen, Saina travelled abroad by herself for the first time, since her parents could not afford to fly with her. She called them several times a day and ran up a huge phone bill. The toughest part of it, besides being alone, was finding food—because Saina was vegetarian.

That same year, during an international tournament in China, Gopi encouraged her to try non-vegetarian food. The Chinese players' diet was protein-rich and Gopi felt it would be good for her. Now Saina eats chicken and fish regularly and enjoys it.

Saina went on to win the Philippines Open, becoming the youngest player in Asia to win the title. Within six years of training with Gopi, her ranking rose to World No. 2. Over the next decade she went from strength to strength, competing at the Super Series, the All England and the BWF Masters Tournament. In 2010, she received the Rajiv Gandhi Khel Ratna Award. She says it was one of her proudest moments.

Illustrated by Tanya Eden

In 2012, Saina became the first Indian woman to win an Olympic medal in badminton. She brought home the bronze. Her mother made her a special treat—aloo parantha—and encouraged her to try for gold the next time.

2013 was a bad year. She didn't win a match for an entire year and was frustrated. She parted ways with Gopichand and moved to Bangalore to train with a new coach, Vimal Kumar, who helped her get back her confidence and start winning again. In 2015, she became the first Indian woman to be ranked World No. 1. A year later, she was awarded the Padma Bhushan. In 2017, Saina moved back to Hyderabad and the Gopichand Badminton Academy.

Saina believes every girl should be encouraged to play sport. In an interview she said, 'Beti Bachao and Beti Padhao is fine, but what about Beti Khilao?'

Around the time that Saina first started training with Gopichand, another little girl was learning to wield the badminton racquet. It happened by chance. Sindhu was tagging along with her father—a national-level volleyball player—to his practice. When they reached the stadium in Hyderabad, she wandered off to the badminton courts. Soon she was playing with some friends.

When her parents saw her enthusiasm for the sport, they introduced her to their friend P. Gopichand. Nine-year-old Sindhu had seen him on TV and was fascinated by his skill. She began training with him a year later and went on to win the Under-10 badminton championships that year.

The Gopichand Academy was 47 km away from Sindhu's home. Her father would drive her there every morning while it was still dark. They would make it in time for her 4.30 a.m. session, six days a week. Sindhu was just ten and the travel was hard on her. By the time she came back from practice, she would be hungry and tired. She could barely finish breakfast before rushing out the door to make it in time for school.

One day, in her hurry to reach school on time, she stuffed all her books into her bag and left. On the way back, she stopped to play a game of badminton. When she finished, her bag was missing. What would she do now? Her exams were due in a few weeks and she had no notes to study from. Her mother scolded her, saying that she would have to work on her notes or she wouldn't be allowed to play. But Sindhu had a tournament coming up in a few months and it was important to practise too. Her parents went to the principal and asked if they could redo the notes on her behalf. The principal agreed, and armed with a new set of notes, Sindhu passed her exam with 82 per cent. A few months later, she won the Under-13 national badminton tournament.

After tenth grade, Sindhu moved to the academy and lived in the hostel there for two years. Her parents eventually moved closer to the academy so that she could have more time at home with them and practise whenever she needed.

In 2013, Sindhu won her first World Badminton Grand Prix title—a gold medal at the Malaysian Open. When she was eighteen, she became the first Indian woman to win a singles medal at the BWF World Championship.

Sindhu was a shy girl. Two years before the 2016 Rio Olympics, her coach said she needed to build aggression. He couldn't so much as make her shout, despite many attempts.

One day, he made her stand in the middle of the court and insisted, 'Shout.' Sindhu burst out crying instead. He kept at it for months. Slowly Sindhu was able to raise her voice and shout and scream and express herself. She is now considered a strong and aggressive player on court.

Gopichand believes that special matches need special training. Eight whole months before the Olympics, Sindhu's phone was confiscated and she was told to give up sugar. She was twenty-one years old then. She went on to win a silver in the singles—the first ever for an Indian woman badminton player.

Sindhu reaches the stadium an hour before every match, to visualise it in advance and discuss strategies and plans with her coach. It's hard to miss her when she is on the court. At 5'11", she towers over almost everyone. It certainly works to her advantage when she smashes. But she's had to put in extra effort to get to the low shots.

Earlier, Sindhu would cry when she lost a tournament. Now the tears come only when she loses a tough match, when she's fighting for the last point at the end of a long match and something goes wrong. She realises that one cannot win all the time.

Like most celebrities, Sindhu is mobbed when she appears in public. When she goes to watch the occasional movie with her family, they enter when the lights are dimmed and leave as soon as it's over.

Today, both Saina and Sindhu walk on to the court with the belief that they can win. Not surprisingly, every time either of them wins a big match, the number of girls who sign up for badminton coaching spikes!

• •

· DIPA KARMAKAR ·

Vaulting to Victory

Six-year-old Dipa looked around the gym, if one could call it that. The dingy room was flooded with rainwater, and cockroaches were running all over the torn mats. She sighed. She was there because her father wanted her to be a gymnast. He was a sportsperson and, unlike many parents who wanted their children to focus only on studies, he and her mother had actively encouraged Dipa to take up a sport.

Dipa's life was very different from that of the other girls in her school. Her headmistress knew she was training for competitive sport, so she allowed Dipa to attend four classes out of seven every day. Dipa had to leave school early for her arduous training sessions with her coach. She had no free time and couldn't have fun playing with her classmates. But all the hard work paid off when, at the age of eight, she won her first medal at the Northeastern Games. She won a gold medal at the balance beam, one of the events in gymnastics. An official at the games recognised her potential and recommended that she train with Bisweshwar Nandi, a gymnast who had once led the national team.

Dipa had flat feet, which put her at a disadvantage. It affected her jumps and landings. But early on, her coach showed her exercises that helped increase the angle of the arch of her feet. Dipa listened to all his instructions and followed them diligently.

As a child, Dipa would get angry with herself if she could not do her best. Coach Nandi would calm her down and advise her to channel her energy into the training. This helped her improve her performance.

Both her coach and her father felt that Dipa was good enough to represent the country at international events. In 2014, she started training for the challenging Produnova routine. Called the vault of death, it involves a dismount of two and a half somersaults off a vaulting horse. Dipa wasn't scared. She trained hard and fearlessly.

Illustrated by Sanchita Jain

That year, Dipa participated in the Glasgow Commonwealth Games. This was the first international competition in which she would be attempting the Produnova. All eyes were on her. She won a bronze medal and became the first woman gymnast from India to win a medal at the Commonwealth Games.

Dipa then started training hard for the Rio Olympics. In general, boys in India have better access to equipment and training facilities than girls. Dipa was determined to prove that she was just as good as any boy. Also, by now, the facilities for gymnasts had improved considerably.

In the three months prior to the Olympics, she practised the Produnova a thousand times. It was physically and mentally exhausting. But both she and her coach had their eyes on a medal. During the Olympic qualifiers, Dipa was placed eighth. By then she had already broken a record by becoming the first Indian woman gymnast to qualify for the Olympics.

On 10 August 2016, Dipa surpassed all expectations and vaulted to fourth place in the Olympics.

Afterwards, disappointed with the result, she said to her coach, 'Now that we haven't got any medals, let's return to India, get into a taxi and go home.'

Coach Nandi then told her that all of India had been following the Olympics with rapt attention, their hopes pinned on Dipa. People who hadn't even heard of the Produnova had watched her execute it with bated breath. She would be going back to a proud nation!

On her return, Dipa was asked who should play her if a movie was made on her life. She laughed and said, 'Someone who can do the Produnova.'

• •

Illustrated by Joanna Mendes

·POORNA MALAVATH·

Girl on the Summit

Poorna was playing kabaddi in the school playground, deep in thought. What would the next month be like? She had just taken an exam for a residential school in a nearby village. Would she get in? She couldn't continue studying in her own village, Pakala, Telangana. There were no classes beyond grade four.

Pakala was far from even a small town. The villagers had to walk a few kilometres to take a bus to the nearest shop. The new school was 40 km away, but Poorna was looking forward to it. Her parents, both agricultural labourers, were also hoping Poorna would get admission. When she did get accepted, her first thought was that she would now be able to eat good food.

Poorna continued to play kabaddi but also grew to love volleyball. Around this time, an Indian Police Services (IPS) officer, R.S. Praveen Kumar, was assigned to oversee and improve the way social welfare residential institutions were run in the area. He started to make positive changes in the living conditions of the students and encouraged sports in all schools. Poorna's physical education instructors took advantage of these new opportunities and selected her for a rock climbing programme.

A hundred and ten students participated in the rock climbing exercise. The mountaineer Shekhar Babu Bachinappai was in charge.

When Poorna saw the imposing 650-foot high Bhongir rock, she was scared. She had never climbed before. It was tough in the beginning, but soon she started enjoying the challenge. As she learnt rappelling and bouldering, her stamina grew. On the basis of her skill and capacity for hard work, Shekhar Babu declared her the star of the five-day training camp.

Poorna then went for an advanced course in Darjeeling. She saw snow for the first time and played in it with great joy. But it was also the first time she was experiencing temperatures below zero. She gradually learnt how to walk in the snow, what to wear, and how to survive.

Her next major challenge was being part of an expedition to Mount Renock in the Kangchenjunga range. The summit was at 17,000 feet and the climb was hard. She knew she had to eat to keep her strength up. But packaged food—bread and jam? She hated it.

After the expedition's success, Poorna continued to train for physical and mental fitness. She learnt yoga and meditation. Shekhar Babu got the trainees to watch inspiring films about mountaineers and taught them mountaineering theory.

Poorna then went to Ladakh for fifteen days. If Darjeeling was cold, Ladakh was freezing. She learnt to pitch a tent and get acclimatised to temperatures as low as minus 32° C. It was tough, but she coped well.

Now Shekhar Babu and Praveen Kumar felt Poorna was ready to climb Mount Everest. They called her parents for permission and told them about the expedition and the dangers involved. While her father, who always encouraged her, told Poorna to go ahead, her mother started to cry—how would her child survive such a difficult trek?

Poorna and a young boy, Anand Kumar, with whom she had trained, flew to Nepal with their coach. First they went to the Everest Base Camp. They started the climb with a support group of fifteen people—including sherpas, a doctor and a cook. Poorna was worried. The mountain was steep; also, it was windy and snowing. She found the climb to Camp One tough. Because of the high altitude, she vomited on the way up. Would she be able to do it? As they climbed higher, she was scared. She saw a dead body lying on the mountain, and was told they had to leave it there; it would be nearly impossible to take it down.

On the morning of 25 May 2014, at 6.30 a.m., Poorna summited Mount Everest. She was thrilled—her hard work and training had paid off! She had carried an Indian flag and a photo of her hero, Dr B.R. Ambedkar, in her pocket—she held these up at the top of Mount Everest.

The team took three days to get back to base camp. When Poorna finally got there, Shekhar Babu told her that she was the youngest girl in history to scale Mount Everest. She was thirteen years and eleven months old at the time.

When Poorna returned home, her mother cried again—this time, they were tears of joy. A rally had been organised for the two mountaineers in Hyderabad. For Poorna this was the happiest moment of her life.

Poorna has since summited Mount Kilimanjaro in Tanzania and Mount Elbrus in Russia. Her mountaineering goal is to climb the seven highest mountains in every continent.

• •

·A READING GUIDE·

What Is Caste?

What if you were told that in your school, you had to do jobs that no one else in your class did, like cleaning the school bathrooms? Or that you couldn't take part in extra-curricular activities or enter certain areas? What if you were punished for no reason? What if no one at school shared their food with you? Or made fun of the food in your tiffin because it wasn't what they ate? What if you were not allowed to befriend or date certain people?

What if you were told that all of this was just because you were born into a 'low caste' family?

Millions of people in India are discriminated against every day. When people believe that they are better than others because they happen to be born into an 'upper caste' Brahmin, Kshatriya or Vaishya family, they believe in the caste system. The caste system in Hinduism originated centuries ago and is prevalent even today. It places power in certain people's hands and denies others their right to equality. Surprisingly, such discrimination has also crept into other religious communities in India.

Some people flaunt their caste by wearing markers like a sacred thread, coloured lines on their foreheads, or a certain type of clothing. They might believe that some people are untouchable and that doing manual or 'unclean' work is the job of other people. They might use separate glasses and plates for household staff, give staff their leftover food, or make them use a different kitchen or a service lift in the building. They might believe that they should only marry people of 'their own kind'. These are a few examples of how people keep the caste system alive, ensuring that society stays divided.

Dalits and some Adivasis are the worst victims of the caste system and many are considered untouchable by the 'upper castes', who make up less than 20 per cent of Indian society.

(With inputs from Malavika Binny and Namit Arora)

Who Is a Devadasi?

There was a time when dancing and music were a big part of Hindu temple rituals to serve the gods. These rituals were performed by women called devadasis, or 'female servants of god', who were attached to specific temples. They were trained from an early age in dance, music and theatre. Many became highly skilled and were the original proponents of a number of complex dance forms, including the Sadir dance. This was later co-opted and embellished to become what is now known as Bharatanatyam.

Devadasis earned money or were alloted land for their performances, and some even supported their families. Sometime in the fourteenth or fifteenth century, their status declined. Young girls, mostly from 'lower castes' and poor homes, were 'married' to a god or a temple. Some were forcibly sent to the temple before attaining puberty, and were subject to atrocities by people from 'upper castes' who were associated with the temple. In some cases, these girls were treated like slaves by the temple priests. Many were forced to serve as prostitutes and slowly a stigma grew around their profession.

In some parts of India, this practice still exists.

(With inputs from Malavika Binny and Namit Arora)

What Does Prostitution Mean?

A prostitute is someone who takes part in sexual activity in return for payment. In most cases, prostitutes are young girls or boys who have been kidnapped and sold to people who make a business out of it. Most of them don't have a right to say no and are controlled by someone who 'manages' them.

There are some who choose to be sex workers and have not been forced to be, or stay, in the trade. But it is their choice and it is wrong to think of them as 'bad' or 'dirty' or 'immoral'.

To call someone a prostitute as an insult is something we should avoid.

(With inputs from Talish Ray)

Understanding Mental Health Issues

A mental health illness is caused by a chemical imbalance or disturbance in some part of the brain. There are many types of mental illness. It can affect anyone—educated and uneducated, men and women, young and old, rich and poor. Some people are very happy for weeks and then suddenly they get very, very sad. Sometimes they can be disruptive and troublesome. This can last for weeks or months. The condition is called bipolar affective disorder.

Some people may be so sad (and for no obvious reason) that they may not be able to do anything for days. This is called depression. Depression can also manifest as an intense preoccupation with physical health. It is very common for depressed children to bunk school and be disinterested in studies because they are unable to concentrate.

Most mental health problems can be treated with medication and therapy. Only 10 per cent of mental health patients require hospitalisation. Families, friends and classmates can play an important role in helping people with mental health disorders. You can start by accepting people the way they are, being patient, non-judgmental, and supportive of their needs. Don't shame people with mental health issues or be critical of their behaviour. Avoid using words like 'psycho', 'mad' or 'crazy'. And remember, mental illness is not the result of 'karma' or personal weaknesses. It's just like any other medical issue. You wouldn't make fun of a cancer patient, would you?

(With inputs from Dr Kishore Kumar, The Banyan)

What Is Puberty?

When humans are a certain age, usually between ten and sixteen, the body undergoes certain changes to attain maturity. Girls become taller, their breasts and reproductive organs develop, they grow armpit, pubic and some facial hair.

As a girl matures, her body starts producing eggs inside the ovaries every month. When a sperm does not fertilize the egg in twenty-four hours, it dies. After fourteen days, the lining of the uterus sheds in the form of blood. This lasts between two and seven days and is called menstruation. It is also called a period.

Boys also mature, just differently. Their voice deepens and they begin to grow body and facial hair. The body also starts preparing for reproduction. The testicles enlarge, as does the penis. The testicles begin producing semen, which carries sperm, and comes out as a whitish fluid from the penis. This process is called ejaculation.

(With inputs from Dr Sangeeta Saksena, Co-Founder, Enfold Trust)

What Does The Word 'Rape' Mean?

Your body belongs to you and no one should do anything that makes you feel uncomfortable.

When someone is violent and penetrates any part of another person's body against their will, even with an object, it is called rape. If someone touches a person inappropriately, or in an unsafe way, here are three safety rules to follow: No – Go – Tell. Say 'No' to the abuser if you can. Go to a safe place when you can. Tell an adult you trust about the abuse.

You can confide in a parent, relative, friend, teacher, or a friend's parent you trust. Keep telling people till you find someone who believes you.

(With inputs from Dr Sangeeta Saksena, Co-founder, Enfold Trust)

Understanding the Concept of LGBTQIA
(Lesbian, Gay, Bisexual, Transgender, Queer, Intersex and Asexual)

Some people believe that men should fall in love only with women and that women should love only men. But people are unique in how they love and are drawn to others.

A 'gay' person is attracted to others of their own gender. A transgender person is someone who does not identify with their birth gender. An intersex person is born with several variations of sex organs and chromosomes.

Language is broadening to become inclusive of people with different sexualities and preferences, and you can look these terms up further.

Same-sex marriage is allowed in over twenty countries, but not yet in India. India recognises a third gender. This includes members of the hijra community, as well as transgender and intersex persons.

None of these terms should be used as an insult.

(With inputs from Danish Shaikh and Harish Iyer)

· BIBLIOGRAPHY ·

1. AMRITA SHER-GIL

Dalmia, Yashodhara. *Amrita Sher-Gil: A Life*.
New Delhi: Penguin Random House, 2013.

Sundaram, Vivan. *Amrita Sher-Gil: A Self-portrait in Letters and Writing*.
Chennai: Tulika Books, 2010.

2. BAMA

Bama, trans. Lakshmi Holmstrom. *Karukku*.
New Delhi: Oxford University Press, 2013.

3. BIRUBALA RABHA

Baruah, Aditya. 'A witch-hunting survivor takes up crusade to save
Assamese women'. TwoCircles, 14 June 2016,
http://twocircles.net/ 2016jun14/1465920216.html, accessed 13 April 2018.

Madhukalya, Amrita. 'The "witches" of Assam: Hunted, beheaded
and raped'. *DNA*, 15 May 2016.
http://www.dnaindia.com/lifestyle/ report-the-witches-of-assam-hunted
beheaded-and-raped-2212383, accessed 12 April 2018.

Raimedhi, Indrani. *My Half of the Sky: 12 Life Stories of Courage*.
New Delhi: Sage Publications, 2015.

www.missionbirubala.com, accessed 12 April 2018.

4. DEVIKA RANI

Sawhney, Rajinder Cary. 'Devika Rani' in *Bollywood's Top 20: Superstars of
Indian Cinema*, ed. Bhaichand Patel.
New Delhi: Penguin Random House, 2016.

5. MUTHULAKSHMI REDDI

Rajeshwari, Krishna. *Dr S. Muthulakshmi Reddi*.
Bengaluru: Sapna Book House, 2006.

Reddi, Muthulakshmi. *Autobiography of Dr (Mrs) S. Muthulakshmi Reddi*.
Chennai: MLJ Press, 1965.

6. ELA R. BHATT

Bhatt, Ela. *We Are Poor But So Many: The Story of Self-Employed Women in India.*
New Delhi: Oxford University Press, 2007.

7. GAURI LANKESH

Gowda, Chandan. *The Way I See It: The Gauri Lankesh Reader.*
New Delhi: Navayana & DC Books, 2017.

8. HOMAI VYARAWALLA

Gadihoke, Sabeena. *India in Focus: Camera Chronicles of Homai Vyarawalla.*
Mumbai: Grantha Corporation, 2010.

9. INDIRA PRIYADARSHINI GANDHI

Gandhi, Indira. *Anand Bhavan Memories.*
New Delhi: Indira Gandhi Memorial Trust, 1989.
——*My Truth.* New Delhi: Orient Paperbacks, 2007.
Ghose, Sagarika. *Indira: India's Most Powerful Prime Minister.*
New Delhi: Juggernaut Books, 2017.
Jayakar, Pupul. *Indira Gandhi: A Biography.*
New Delhi: Penguin Books, 2000.
Kapoor, Coomi. *The Emergency: A Personal History.*
New Delhi: Penguin Random House, 2016.
Sahgal, Nayantara. *Indira Gandhi: A Tryst with Power.*
New Delhi: Penguin Books, 2012.
Tully, Mark & Jacob, Satish. *Amritsar: Mrs Gandhi's Last Battle.*
New Delhi: Rupa Publications, 2006.

10. IROM SHARMILA CHANU

Bhonsle, Anubha. *Mother, Where's My Country: Looking for Light in the Darkness of Manipur.*
New Delhi: Speaking Tiger, 2016.
https://iromsharmilachanu.wordpress.com, accessed 13 April 2018.
Mehrotra, Deepti Priya. *Burning Bright: Irom Sharmila and the Struggle for Peace in Manipur.*
New Delhi: Penguin Books, 2009.

11. J. JAYALALITHAA

Vaasanthi. *Amma: Jayalalithaa's Journey from Movie Star to Political Queen.*
New Delhi: Juggernaut Books, 2016.

12. KIRAN MAZUMDAR-SHAW

Singh, Seema. *Mythbreaker: Kiran Mazumdar-Shaw and the Story of Indian Biotech*.
New Delhi: HarperCollins, 2016.

13. LEILA SETH

Seth, Leila. *On Balance: An Autobiography*.
New Delhi: Penguin Books, 2007.

14. MANGTE CHUNGNEIJANG MARY KOM

Kom, Mary & Serto, Dino. *Unbreakable: An Autobiography*.
New Delhi: HarperCollins, 2013.

15. KUMARI MAYAWATI

Bose, Ajoy. *Behenji: A Political Biography of Mayawati*.
New Delhi: Penguin Books, 2012.
Dixit, Neha. 'The Mission Inside Mayawati's Battle for Uttar Pradesh'.
The Caravan. 1 February 2017.
http://www.caravanmagazine.in/reportage/mayawatibattle-for-uttar-pradesh-mission, accessed 13 April 2018.

16. M.S. SUBBULAKSHMI

George, T.J.S. *M.S. Subbulakshmi: A Definitive Biography*.
New Delhi: Aleph Book Company, 2016.
Vishwanathan, Lakshmi. *Kunjamma: Ode to a Nightingale*.
New Delhi: Roli Books, 2003.

17. RANI LAKSHMIBAI

Misra, Jaishree. *Rani*. New Delhi: Penguin Books, 2008.
Versaikar, Vishnu Bhatt Godshe, trans. Mrinal Pande. *1857: The Real Story of the Great Uprising*.
New Delhi: HarperCollins, 2011.

18. RUKHMABAI RAUT

Chandra, Sudhir. *Enslaved Daughters: Colonialism, Law and Women's Rights*.
New Delhi: Oxford University Press, 2008.
Rappaport, Helen. *Victoria: The Heart and Mind of a Young Queen*.
London: HarperCollins, 2017.

19. RUKMINI DEVI ARUNDALE

Samson, Leela. *Rukmini Devi: A Life*.
New Delhi: Penguin Books, 2010.
https://www.youtube.com/watch?v=1Hq9YRhm_1Y, accessed 13 April 2018.
https://www.youtube.com/watch?v=aHYQGyoU2Ko, accessed 13 April 2018.
https://www.youtube.com/watch?v=2gpTmVv-esQ, accessed 13 April 2018.
https://www.youtube.com/watch?v=7-bejYWq7CY accessed 13 April 2018.
https://www.youtube.com/watch?v=k6fkZpzcjLI, accessed 13 April 2018.

20. SANIA MIRZA

Mirza, Sania. *Ace Against Odds*.
New Delhi: HarperCollins, 2015.

21. SAVITRIBAI PHULE

Mani, Braj Ranjan & Sardar, Pamela. *A Forgotten Liberator: The Life and Struggle of Savitribai Phule*.
New Delhi: Good Word, 2008.
Sharma, Ruchika. 'The First Feminist of India' in *Equal Halves: Famous Indian Wives*, ed. Annie Zaidi.
New Delhi: Juggernaut Books, 2017.

22. SHAH BANO BEGUM

Akhtar, Saleem. *Shah Bano Judgement in Islamic Perspective: A Socio-Legal Study*.
New Delhi: Kitab Bhawan, 1994.
Engineer, Asghar Ali. *The Shah Bano Controversy*.
New Delhi: Sangam Books, 1987.
Khan, Saeed. 'My mother was wronged, gravely wronged'. *Hindustan Times*, 12 November 2011.
https://www.hindustantimes.com/india/my-mother-was-wrongedgravely-wronged/story-uOLF1nso2P9zX9TwzPB0dM.html, accessed 13 April 2018.
Mody, Zia. *10 Judgements That Changed India*.
New Delhi: Penguin Books, 2013.

23. TEESTA SETALVAD

Setalvad, Teesta. *Foot Soldiers of the Constitution: A Memoir*.
New Delhi: Leftword Books, 2017.

24. LAKSHMI SAHGAL & MRINALINI SARABHAI

Ali, Subhashini. 'A life in service'.

http://www.indiaseminar.com/2004/540/540%20subhashini%20ali.
htm, accessed 13 April 2018.

Sarabhai, Mrinalini. *Voice of the Heart: An Autobiography*.

New Delhi: HarperCollins, 2005.

25. LATA MANGESHKAR & ASHA BHOSLE

Bharatan, Raju. *Asha Bhosle: A Musical Biography*.

New Delhi: Hay House, 2016.

——'How Lata Mangeshkar proved Dilip Kumar wrong', Rediff,

http://specials.rediff.com/movies/2008/jul/07slid1.htm,accessed 13 April 2018.

Deora, Mohan & Shah, Rachana. *On Stage with Lata*.

New Delhi: HarperCollins, 2017.

Kabir, Nasreen Munni. *Lata Mangeshkar in Her Own Voice*.

New Delhi: Niyogi Books, 2009.

26. SAINA NEHWAL & P.V. SINDHU

Nehwal, Saina. *Playing to Win*.

New Delhi: Penguin Books, 2012.

https://www.youtube.com/watch?v=YLxQ1woar4A, accessed 13 April 2018.

https://www.youtube.com/watch?v=x_GshFvil20, accessed 13 April 2018.

Sindhu, P.V. 'P.V. Sindhu'. *Tinkle,* Vol. 679, Mumbai: ACK Media, 2017

https:// www.youtube.com/watch?v=bWRyg5G6rrk, accessed 13 April 2018.

https://www.youtube.com/watch?v=tvADU5ty5zI, accessed 13 April 2018.

https://www.indiatoday.in/india-today-conclave-2018/video/
indiatoday-conclave-2018-the-3-decisions-that-changed-pv-sindhu-
s-career-1185761-2018-03-09, accessed 13 April 2018.

THE ARTISTS

Ayesha Broacha paints, and is a
photographer and marathon runner.
Insta: @ayeshabroacha
Email: ayeshabroachaart@gmail.com

Aarti Malik is an illustrator and UX/UI
designer. Painting is therapy for her.
Insta: aartimalik
Email: malik.arti10@gmail.com

Alia Sinha is a self-taught artist and enjoys the
intersection of theatre, books and art.
Insta: @minorgrace
Email: moontuner@gmail.com

Anjul Dandekar is a self-taught artist who
loves to tell stories through her art.
Insta: @anjul_dandekar
Email: Anjuldandekar2777@gmail.com

Aparajita Ninan is a visualiser and
illustrator. While she was on this project, she had
a baby.
Insta: @appuninan
Email: aparajitaninan@gmail.com

Ayangbe Mannen is a self-taught artist and illustrator, and is constantly experimenting with different techniques and styles.
Email: ayangbemannen@gmail.com
Website: www.ayangbe.com

Bhavya Kumar is a student and freelance illustrator who intends working in the field of education to explore the pedagogic role of graphic narratives.
Insta: @theawkwardfreelancer
Website: www.theawkwardfreelancer.com

Girija Hariharan is an engineer turned muralist. She loves to paint doors and walls.
Email: 2flatbrush@gmail.com
Website: www.2flatbrush.com

Joanna Mendes is a freelance illustrator who loves to observe people and bring their gestures and expressions into her art.
Insta: @jontupontu
Email: mendes.joan@gmail.com

Osheen Siva is an illustrator, artist and graphic designer whose major influences include Alan Moore, James Jean and Egon Schiele.
Email: osheensiva@gmail.com
Website: https://www.behance.net/osheensiva

Priya Kuriyan is an illustrator and comics maker. She is happiest when filling her sketchbooks with strange caricatures of people in places she travels to.
Email: priyakuriyan@gmail.com

Priyanka Tampi is a recluse who lives in her pyjamas, daydreaming, doodling and writing funny poems.
Insta: @tampipriyanka
Email: tampipriyanka@gmail.com

Priyanka Paul is one of the youngest illustrators in this book. her work revolves around themes of social justice and activism. She is also a poet.
Insta: @artwhoring
Email: priyankapauly@gmail.com

Rae Zachariah is an illustrator and graphic designer who is inspired by music. She loves injecting humour into everything she does.
Insta: @raezack
Email: Raezack@gmail.com

Sanchita Jain is a communication designer. Illustrating helps her channel her anxieties and give voice to her geekiness.
Email: sanchitajain17@gmail.com

Sayalee Karkare is a freelance writer and illustrator based in Boulder, Colorado. She drinks way too much coffee and wishes her hair were naturally blue.
Insta: @sayachanaar
Email: sayalee.karkare@gmail.com

Sheena Deviah is a corporate clown turned illustrator and hand poke tattoo artist.
Insta: @sheenadeviahaha
Email: sheenadeviah@gmail.com

Shikha Nambiar is a corporate lawyer turned illustrator who lives with her feisty cat, Yoda.
Insta: @chicabeingme
Email: sunnyskiestarryeyes@gmail.com

Shivanee Harshey is a designer who prefers visuals over words, imagination over execution and teams over individuals.
Insta: @harsheyshivanee
Email: shivanee.harshey@gmail.com

Shruti Prabhu is a graphic designer, illustrator, travel blogger and tech nerd who lives in her happy bubble.
Email: shruti.prabhu87@gmail.com
Website: http://shrutiprabhu.com/

Siddhangana Karmakar is a self-taught artist who spends her weekends drawing in cafes and parks on her iPad.
Insta: @siddhanganart
Email: siddhanganak@gmail.com

Sudeepti Tucker is a freelance illustrator who likes to explore ideas of feminism and identity through her art.
Insta: @sudeepti.tucker
Email: sudeepti.tucker@gmail.com

Suhana Medappa discovered painting late in life but is now trying to make it as a nine-to-five graphic designer.
Insta: @suhanamedappa
Email: suhanamedappa@gmail.com

Sujata Bansal loves drawing faces and is a self-taught artist.
Email: sujatabansal@yahoo.com

Tanya Eden is a visual storyteller who believes in standing up for social causes.
Insta: @tanyaedenart
Email: tanyaeden92@gmail.com

Tara Anand is one of the youngest artists in the book. Her work is deeply influenced by literature, activism and history. She likes to make zines.
Email: taraanandillustration@gmail.com
Website: taraanandart.com

Teju Jhaveri is an illustrator and graphic designer who loves food, puppies and the *Lord of the Rings*.
Email: teju.jhaveri@gmail.com
Website: www.windingroad.design

· ACKNOWLEDGEMENTS ·

This book has been my most ambitious project with its multiple moving parts.

I had to do sixty-two interviews—and it was not easy. I had to locate my subjects, write to them or their agents, and chase them for months on end for a half-hour slot. The last interview took place barely ten days before the book was sent to press, when P.V. Sindhu was headed to the airport shortly after the All England. I read thirty-seven books, watched umpteen YouTube videos and read multiple web articles. I worked with twenty-six young artists. All this in six months.

I have many people to thank. First, the two people who believed in this book and made it happen—Karthika V.K. and Gautam Padmanabhan. Karthika has played a crucial role in shaping every book of mine with her tough love and terrifying eraser. This book would not be the beauty it is without her attention and care.

I sent every piece of art to Ajitha G.S. for critical comment and had long discussions with her on the difficult icons. The book owes a lot to her. Also, to Vishwajyoti Ghosh for the stunning design, Shrutika Mathur for patiently putting up with every edit, and Sonakshi Singh for making it all so pretty.

Ayesha Broacha, classmate and art director, whom I would hound from 4 a.m. to midnight pretty much every day. She says I 'gave her grief' but I think it worked both ways!

Nimmy Chacko, my editor, who worked intensely on the book to fine-tune it for a young audience. Surprisingly, we didn't meet during the editing—we only communicated via Google drive folder exchanges.

All the women in this book who took the time to speak with me: Anshu Jamsenpa, Aruna Roy, Bama, Barkha Dutt, Bhanwari Devi, Dayamani Barla, Ela R. Bhatt, Indira Jaising, Karamjyoti Dalal, Kiran Mazumdar–Shaw, Medha Patkar, Mithali Raj, Poorna Malavath, Ritu

Dalmia, Sharda Ugra, Soni Sori, Sudha Varghese, Sunita Narain, Tessy Thomas, Teesta Setalvad, P.V. Sindhu, Dipa Karmakar, Rashida Bi, Champa Devi Shukla, Vandana Gopikumar, Vaishnavi Jayakumar and Gauri Sawant.

The relatives of some of the women, who I was in touch with for the stories: Kavitha Lankesh, Banarasi Lal Chawla, Bibhaas Amonkar, Shantum Seth, Ina Puri, Shamya Dasgupta, V. Srinivasan, Imran Mirza, Siddiqa Begum, Subhashini Ali, Mallika Sarabhai.

The many people who helped with connects and inputs: Anandi Ishwaran, Dr V. Shanta, Neha Dixit, Meenu Handa, Senthil Kumar, Sandeep Unnithan, Anubha Bhonsle, Rana Safvi, Chatura Padaki, Sidharth Bhatia, Geetu Vaid, Indira Raimedhi, Dr Praveen Kumar, Nasreen Munni Kabir, Jaishree Misra, Sabeena Gadihoke, Ayesha Sood, Baba Aadhav, Kishalay Bhattacharjee, Sanjay Pugalia, Satyajit Sarna, Radhakrishnan R.K. and Anil Padmanabhan.

Swaty Singh Malik, who tenaciously organised an elusive interview for me.

Yashwanth Biyyala, Sharba Tasneem, Anisha Gupta, who managed to sneak me into the calendars of the sportswomen.

Dr Sangeeta Saksena, Malavika Binny, Dr Kishore Kumar, Namit Arora, Danish Sheikh, Harish Iyer, Talish Ray, who provided expert inputs for the notes section.

A shout-out to Kavita Srivastava of PUCL, a woman whose name has been bookmarked for the next volume. GoSports Foundation, which has supported many sportspersons, including Dipa Karmakar. Former class-mate Ramya Rangarajan, who set the ball rolling by introducing me to Senior Advocate Sanjay Parikh, who gave me my first lead.

Rashmi Dhanwani, Irna Sayeed, Bonita Vaz-Shimray and Sanket Avlani, who introduced me to the artists. All the artists who formed a part of this book. And all those who were almost part of it.

Nisha Agrawal, Tejas Patel and Shivanee Harshey of Oxfam India: you folks are the best!

My incredible family: Peggy maami (my special editor as always); Raja maamu, whose question to me every evening was, 'So how many stories are done today?'; Arjun, my brother, who would always text back with 'I want this poster' or 'I want this tee shirt' when I sent him artwork.

Aradhana and Arianna, my special nieces and human barometers for gauging how tweens would react to the writing. Their feedback ranged from, 'Bua, that was inspiring, Bua, that is sad, Bua, this makes me angry' to just 'WHY?'. My nephews Adianta, Adrish and Kaivalya, just for being cute and being around. Aditya, Nita, Abhinav, Joanna, to whom this book is dedicated.

And the people responsible for creating Microsoft Excel, you are my heroes. I could not have managed this project without my countless spreadsheets!

Please continue to follow the project on www.likeagirl.co.in and send us pictures and stories of yourself (if you are a kid) or of children (if you are a parent or educator) reading the book. We would love to upload them.

We will also upload them on our instagram handle @likeagirl.co.in. Follow us for all the action!

About the Author

Aparna Jain is a leadership coach and an advocate for diversity and inclusion in the workplace.

She is the author of *Own It: Leadership Lessons from Women Who Do*, which was awarded a Laadli Prize and was shortlisted for the Tata Literature Live Business Book Award 2016. She is also the author of *The Sood Family Cookbook* (2013).

HOW TO RAISE A FEMINIST CHILD

Teach boys to be self-reliant.	Encourage boys to express a range of emotions.	Encourage girls to have a career path.

Encourage children to pursue activities they enjoy.	Read books, watch movies with women role models.	Demonstrate equality and respect in relationships through your behaviour.

ART PATRON
- Like a Girl -

ऑक्सफैम इंडिया
OXFAM
India

 Oxfamindia   Oxfam_india   Oxfamindia

Illustrated by Tara Anand

Questions I Have